Jón Guðmundsson lærði's True Account and the Massacre of Basque Whalers in Iceland in 1615

Edited by Xabier Irujo and Viola Miglio

Center for Basque Studies
University of Nevada, Reno

This book was published with the generous
financial assistance of the Basque government.

**Jón Guðmundsson lærði's True Account and
the Massacre of Basque Whalers in Iceland in 1615**

Center for Basque Studies
University of Nevada, Reno
Reno, Nevada 89557
http://basque.unr.edu

ISBN: 9781935709831

Conference Papers Series, no. 13
Series Editor: Xabier Irujo
Center for Basque Studies
University of Nevada, Reno
Reno, Nevada 89557
http://basque.unr.edu

Contents

Jón Guðmundsson lærði's True Account and the Massacre of Basque Whalers in Iceland in 1615

Xabier Irujo
University of the Nevada, Reno
Viola Miglio
University of California, Santa Barabara

A cudgel smashed Lazarus's head
and then Pedro's brow.
A cut made by a sharp and thick pollaxe
crossed his face under the eyes;
Then quickly again close to his heart,
he was passed through with the spike.
He fell asleep into death's embrace
that night.
The youngster's head was cleft asunder
and his legs cut off at the knees;
Those three companions
defended themselves bravely,
but died all the same that night.

"The one that told the story saw all of this from the door of the house" wrote Jón Guðmundsson, author of these verses. Then there were another three men down by the smithy, "the barber, a young man, was sleeping, as well as the boy that took care of smoking fish and the one who took care of the washing." The punitive expedition men ripped the roof off the house, but the men inside defended themselves more than expected. After their deaths, all the men were stripped naked, brought to the cliffs, tied together and thrown into the sea.

On the night of September 20, 1615, the eve of the feast of St. Matthew, an expedition of Basque whalers lost their ships in a fjord near Trékyllisvík during a terrible storm. This led to a series of events that culminated in the October massacre, with the horrible death of more than thirty-two seamen at hands of the islanders. The Basque mariners bodies, dismembered, would not be buried. However, not all Icelanders saw that massacre with good eyes. One of them, Jón Guðmundsson, better known as Jón lærði (1574–1658) or "the wise man", wrote an essay on those events in defense of the victims titled "Sönn frásaga" (The true story).

Four hundred years later, on April 20, 2015, an international conference investigated various aspects of this tragic episode of the history of Iceland and the Basque Country. The academic meeting took place at the National Library of Iceland with the participation of experts from all over the world. The program, commemorating the fourth centenary of the massacre of Basque whalers in Iceland, was sponsored by the Government of Gipuzkoa and the Government of Iceland and organized by the Etxepare Institute, the Basque-Finnish Association, the Center for Basque Studies of the University of Nevada, Reno and the Barandiaran Chair of the University of California, Santa Barbara.

At the official opening of the conference, the head of the National Library of Iceland, Ingibjörg Steinunn Sverrisdóttir, former President of Iceland and UNESCO ambassador for the defense of languages, welcomed the persons attending and appreciated the publication of a new edition of Jón Guðmundsson's manuscript in Basque, Spanish, English, and Icelandic. In fact, within the framework of the conference three new publications were presented as an effort to disseminate the results of various researcg regarding the massacre and, in general, around the mostly peaceful Basque-Icelandic economic, cultural, and social interaction during the course of the seventeenth century.

The book that the reader has now in his hands is the fourth work published as a result of the celebration of this conference.

The present volume opens with an article by Alvaro Aragon and Alberto Angulo, professors of the University of the Basque Country, on the "Basque Whale Hunting and Cod Fishery in the North Atlantic in the Sixteenth–Eighteenth Centuries". Aragon and Angulo analyze how despite challenging political, economic, and strategic obstacles, Basques fishers and whale hunters organized North Atlantic expeditions for almost five centuries. They did not hesitate to move to northernmost new grounds when whales or cod were scarce in other waters or when political obstacles emerged. According to the referred authors, one of the keys to their success was the unique organization of their work based on the sharing of ships, crews, captains, freighters, and capital. When there was a shortage of means or when political problems such as wars arose in the international arena, Basque fishermen organized their North Atlantic expeditions together and they were in general very success-ful: it is estimated that the Basque whalers captured some 25,000 to 40,000 whales between 1530 and 1610. All this was possible in part because Basque fishermen were free men, owners of their time, their work, and their working tools and capable of carrying out the commercial missions on their own, since self-government ensured universal equality of their subjects at home and abroad and mobility along the seas. Regarding the internal organization of these intercontinental enterprises, authors emphasize the influence of the Fishermen's Guilds culture: fishing had a great tradition and a long history in the Basque Country, and fishermen were governed in their commercial enterprises in accordance with the legal patterns of their guilds when they embarked. These organizational rules were therefore among the reasons for the success of the Basque whalers. Also, despite the fact that, during the early modern age, economy was divided by the boundaries of the states, more than often international political barriers meant bridges instead of obstacles for the Basques, connecting people, business, and economies beyond political boundaries and administrative limitations.

Following the organizational analysis of Aragon and Angulo, William Douglass, professor emeritus of the University of Nevada, Reno, offers a deep analysis of the Basque maritime expeditions in his chapter "The Ubiquitous Basque Mariners." Basque maritime history precedes the sixteen century by almost three hundred years when Basque vessels plied the trade routes of both the European Atlantic littoral and the Mediterranean. In the fourteenth century Basques maintained a "House of Bizkaia" in Bruges to facilitate their North Atlantic trade and were negotiating commercial treaties with England. In the service of both the Portuguese and Castilian crowns, they participated in the exploration of North African waters and the equatorial African Atlantic beyond. Antonio de Nebrija, a contemporary of Christopher Columbus, stated that "those who resided in the County of Bizkaia and the Province of Gipuzkoa are people wise in the art of navigation and forceful in naval battles, and they have ships and appurtenances for them, and in these three regards they are better informed than any other nation of the world." By 1615 Basques had circumnavigated the world and it is certain that by the early 1500s Basque whalers and cod fishermen maintained seasonal land operations during summers in Newfoundland to process their catch before returning to their homeland in the autumn. Douglass's chapter focuses on the Basque maritime technological innovations that were fundamental in the development of the vessels that facilitated long-range probes of the planet's vast oceans and permitted Basque sailors to reach the coast of Iceland at the beginning of the seventeenth century.

After these two introductory chapters on the Basque maritime expeditions, "Baskavígin: The Massacre of Basque Whalers" by Tapio Koivukari and Xabier Irujo, director of the Center for Basque Studies at the University of Nevada, Reno, is a study of the slaughter of the Basque whalers in Iceland in the autumn of 1615. As both authors put it, this is not a black-and-white story but rather an Icelandic saga where incidents seem to run inevitably toward an open conflict and a tragic end. Baskavígin, the slaughter of the Basque whalers in Iceland, may be understood as a conflict between competing stories, the stories which people told to each other about themselves as individuals, families, classes, or ethnic groups or followers of a certain religion, and the stories they learned about others. In seventeenth century Iceland 90 percent of the farmers were tenants and landless workers were obliged to hire themselves out to a farm and, on the other hand, the authorities had to find a place to stay for everyone. Lutheran ethics confirmed this and, society was a network of mutual duties. Also, Iceland had undergone harsh years when foreign pirates reached places like Vestmannaeyjar and Patreksfjörður during the late sixteenth century spreading fear for foreign pirates and distant people. Icelanders lived plagued with the three Fs—famine, fear and frustration—and, the stories Icelanders told to among themselves about the proud champions and Vikings in Icelandic sagas offered a humiliating contrast for contemporary stagnation, fear, and shortage. The Basques, on the other hand, had been experiencing a golden era of whaling in Terranova (Newfoundland) and its decline. The whaling know-how had leaked out when Dutch and Englishmen had also begun whaling and Basques were trying harder, anxious to find new whaling waters. In this historical context, an Icelandic magistrate, Ari Magnússon of Ögur who had illegally made a little fortune out of the whaler's profits probably also had his reasons to prove himself to his superiors and tenants. After the terrible storm of late September 1615 he declared the Basques outlaws at the court assembly in Súðavík, basically not because of what they had done, but because of what they might do or what they might declare. And a terrible hunt for human beings began.

Following the study of the massacre by Tapio Koivukari and Xabier Irujo, Helgi Þorláksson, history professor at the University of Iceland, delves into the roots of violence regarding the incident of 1615 in his article "Atrocious Icelanders versus Basques: Unexpected Violence or Not?" As the author expresses, Icelanders have often wondered why their ancestors in 1615 treated Basque whalers in such a horrific way, brutally slaughtering many of them and maltreating their corpses. Icelanders today like to see their ancestors in 1615 as we believe Icelandic peasants were in later times, peace loving, hospitable toward strangers, never harming other people on purpose. However, the same does not apply to Iceland around 1600; peasants sometimes fought outside churches on Sundays, carried knives, and would wound their enemies. This is not surprising: the Icelandic society was a feuding society from times immemorial and, until around 1575, manslaughter was not uncommon among the upper layers of society. Killing in revenge took place in cases when those who felt that they had been seriously offended and their honor been tarnished wanted to wash it by killing the offender. However, in the late Middle Ages and until around 1575 only those who could afford to pay a round sum in fines to the king for the act of killing did this. Homicides or instances of manslaughter in revenge were not uncommon in Iceland until around 1575, when they came to an end because of royal disapproval. But as pointed out above, the Icelandic society was still a feuding society around 1615 and the Basques were treated as animals when they were killed and their corpses mutilated. Why were they treated like this? Jón Guðmunds-son expressed that their bodies were maltreated to mock them. Such groups of men, seen as hostile outsiders, did not necessarily have to be foreign, and could very well be domestic groups of thieves and other malefactors, as they were, for instance, in 1545. In addition, bodies of convicts could be dismembered or quartered, as happened to a famous murderer in 1596, whose body parts were spiked, stuck on sticks or poles for display. Something similar occurred in 1635. Professor Þorláksson argues in his chapter that to treat the Basques like animals was intended to convey meaning: they were seen as guilty, trespassers of the boundaries between culture and nature. The expressions used for them, like strákur, suggest that they were seen as guilty outsiders. Accordingly, they were dishonored, stripped of their clothing, quartered, and denied Christian burials. Thus, they were treated as animals.

As the prologists of Baskavígin: The Massacre of Basque Whal-ers (Euskal Erria, Montevideo, 2015) express, Jón Guðmundsson's report on the massacre predates the first deontological codes of journalism by various centuries, but nonetheless he reported the facts following the main principles of the journalistic practice. His intention was to report in an objective way by contrasting and comparing various sources of information and diligently looking for all available sources of information. Guðmundsson avoided making value judgments and carefully filtered the collected information, paying much attention to eyewitnesses' direct accounts. He understood that there is always more than one version of the events and always refused to accept any personal benefits for his journalistic activity. Furthermore he respected the identity of those involved in the massacre by omitting names from the report and did not reveal some of the most revolting details of the slaughter. Finally he wrote the report immediately after the events occurred in 1616 even when it could be used against him, as it was.

Naturalist and writer Hjörleifur Guttormsson studies the footprints of this exceptional writer in Fljótsdalshérað and Bjarnarey in his chapter "In the Footsteps of Jón lærði (the Learned)." Guttormsson studies the journey of Jón Guðmundsson from his arrival in Fljótsdalshérað, East Iceland, in 1632 to his death in 1658. The author provides a comparative study of the natural landscapes in the East and Northwest, were Guðmundsson originally came from will be made because exact records are not available. The author also analyzes and provides illustrations of the archaeological sites from the farmsteads where Guðmundsson lived during his stay in the East will be shown and focuses on the decade from 1640 to 1650, the most fruitful period of Guðmundsson as a writer. As the author demonstrates through examples from Guðmundsson's manuscripts together with some original drawings of whales and other creatures from his Natural History of Iceland, part of his writing were made by request of Bishop Brynjólfur Sveinsson. The author finally focuses with some references to Guðmundsson's facets as painter and craftsman and his work of decoration of the local church at Hjaltastaður were he was buried alongside with his wife Sigríður.

Following Guttormsson's exploration of Guðmundsson's life and cultural environment, independent literary scholar and member of the Reykjavik Academy Viðar Hreinsson studies the phenomenon of violence, relation of power, interests, and truth on the various accounts of the Slayings of the Basques in his chapter "Violence, Power Relations, Interests, and Truth: On the Various Accounts of the Spánverjavíg." According to the author, Jón Guðmundsson's account of the slayings of the Basques is the best known account of that event, but there exists also a substantial amount of poetry and official documents that help illuminating the story from different angles, such as the "Spanish verses" by reverend Ólafur Jónsson's, the "Víkinga rímur," and Jón Guðmundsson's semi-autobiographical poem "Fjölmóður." The author compares the different accounts and their various contextual aspects, such as point of view, personal and social interests, and power relations, in order to shed some light on the credibility of all these different accounts.

Dr. Ólína Kjerulf Þorvarðardóttir, writer and member of several parliamentary committees, studies Jón Guðmundsson's exile and destiny in her chapter "The Fate of the First Icelandic Journalist Jón the Learned: The Interaction of Man and Society in the Era of Sorcery-fear and Premature Justice in the First Half of the Seventeenth century." In his essay, "True Account of the Shipwrecks and Slayings of the Spaniards" (Sönn frásaga af spænskra manna skipbrotum og slagi), Jón Guðmundsson "lærði" wrote the only document of defense for the shipwrecked Basque whalers that were killed in the West Fjords in 1615 and his manuscript cost him his livelihood. Dr. Þorvarðardóttir studies how by his writing he stirred up the wrath and anger of the county sheriff Ari Magnússon in Ögur, responsible for the killing of the Basques. As a result, Guðmundsson fled from West Fjords in midwinter, leaving behind his wife and children and heading to exile. For the rest of his life he was somewhat an outlaw in his own country, persecuted for witchcraft, disrespected, and expelled from society albeit living within it. But who was this man in fact? Was he one of a kind? Did he ever have a chance to "fit in" his own society in the era of sorcery-fear and premature justice in the first half of the seventeenth century? Dr. Þorvarðardótti shed light into these aspects of Guðmundsson's difficult life.

Einar G. Pétursson, professor emeritus of the University of Iceland, studies Jón Guðmundsson's life after he wrote his true account in defense of the Basques in his chapter "Jón Guðmundsson lærði's Sönn frásaga and its repercussions on his life; his stay on Snæfellsnes and his reputation there and later." According to professor Pétursson, Guðmundsson was born in 1574 in Ófeigsfjörður at Strandir in the northwest of Iceland. He grew up in a bookish family and as a young man he copied a number of books, including the Saga of Bishop Guðmundur Arason and a printed gospel book that he decorated with beautiful initials. Jón lærði was also known for his skill as a painter and carver of walrus ivory. Moreover, in 1611–1612 Guðmundsson wrote poems to exorcise ghosts (still extant), the first of them entitled Fjandafæla (Demon Deterrant).

Dr. Pétursson explains that when in 1615 the county sheriff Ari Magnússon in Ögur had some Basques killed Guðmundsson not only refused to participate, but wrote a booklet about the event entitled Sönn frásaga… or A True Account as a result or which he had to flee to Snæfellsnes, where he lived until 1627, supported by the relatives of Guðbrandur Thorlaksson, Bishop of Hólar, who was also the father-in-law of Ari Magnússon. In those years Guðmundsson compiled the Grænlands annál (A chronicle of Greenland) for the scholars at Hólar, and also had contact with scholars in Skálholt. In 1627 the priest Gudmundur Einarsson composed a work called Hugrás (An essay) in response to Fjandafæla, opposing its teachings concerning the origins of demons. Gudmundur's conclusion was that the poem would not scare away demons but rather attract them. As a result, for the next few years Guðmundsson had no fixed homestead, and was sentenced to outlawry in 1631 for a magical handbook he was accused of having written. He went to the eastern part of Iceland and to Copenhagen in 1636, where he was interrogated by the University Council in the spring of 1637. The conclusion was that the case should be reopened in Iceland. There the previous sentence of outlawry was confirmed, though in fact Jón Guðmundsson was allowed to return to eastern Iceland, where he lived to his death in 1658.

Pétursson depicts how in Guðmundsson's last years, the most learned man in Iceland, Brynjólfur Sveinsson, Bishop at Skálholt, encouraged him to write many works, mostly about the old pre-

Christian religion and beliefs of the Nordic people, because the bishop himself intended to write a book about Nordic paganism. In spite of the accusation of witchcraft, which appears not to have bothered the bishop, Jón lærði's reputation for learning was undiminished.

The book closes with the chapter "The Basque Sea in Seventeenth-Eighteenth century texts" by professors Aurélie Arcocha-Scarcia and Mari Jose Olaziregi. The authors have studied the representation of whaling and the maritime world in the Basque literature. As professor Arcocha-Scarcia puts it, some Basque texts of the seventeenth and eighteenth centuries essentially reflect those dangerous sea voyages of sailors hunting whales, fishing cod off the coast of Newfoundland, the St. Lawrence Estuary, South Labrador, indicating how whale hunting and cod fishing require specific instruments and distinct and specialized techniques in defined areas. We know that this context is inseparable from the hazards of politics and of wars between different powers. Politics and religion, we should add— including the eight religion wars that occurred between 1562 and 1598 in France—had a major impact on the production and spread of the religious books and also, on the navigation books to be sold in the ports of the Atlantic coast. The authors first focus on two nonliterary texts, among them the Basque language ship's log by the pilot Captain Pierre Detxeberri, nicknamed "Dorre," who was also a cartographer for Governor Parat of Placentia in 1698 that raises questions about the hypotext written in French, and also about the circulation and spread of the book in Aquitaine where La Rochelle printers who published nautical books had to use clever strategies to make financial profit from selling them, for instance, in Bordeaux. Following this study, the authors analyze an archival document from 1732 that sheds light on the importance of the harpoon business in whaling in 1732. Official policies and cross-border collaborations could be established when there was a shortage of that specific skill on one and/or the other side of the Pyrenean border (as is the case here with the chronic lack of harpooners on the Labourdin side under the French crown). Lastly, both authors study specific literary representations that appear in Basque in The Series of Prayers for the Sea (Bordeaux, 1627), by the religious poet Joanes Etxeberri de

Ciboure, and in four manuscripts found in a song book perhaps made by several compilers and/or authors in a stretch of time from 1714 (after the Treaty of Utrecht) until the early 1800s, or in a broader temporal space than just 1789 to which these texts usually refer. As the authors conclude, the representation of the maritime world in Basque classic texts is necessarily inscribed in a context where other fragments of texts, including those in Basque, meet, including hypotexts like the Odyssey, biblical texts of the Old and New Testament, and sacred history, cosmographies, and legendary voyages to the lands of the North and West.

Four hundred years have passed since a group of peasants around Hólmavik killed a number of Basque whalers. To remember the dead and to strengthen ties between the two nations, a five-day program conference was held in Reyjkavik as well as in the Northern Fjords and in the town of Hólmavik itself close from the places where these events took place. After the international conference and several cultural events, on Wednesday April 22, the last day of winter, President of Gipuzkoa Martin Garitano and the Icelandic Minister of Education and Culture Illugi Gunnarsson spoke at the ceremony that took place in Hólmavik. Following their words, professor Xabier Irujo and the director of the Museum of Witchcraft of Hólmavik Magnús Rafnsson merged in a symbolic embrace; the first in the name of the whalers and the second, as a descendant of the native. It was more than a hug that symbolized the idea that we should not forget the past but learn from it, building bridges and looking with positive will to the future by bringing to memory those who died and promoting debate and research on this and other similar events that have taken place all over the world.

At the occasion, West Fjords district commissioner Jónas Guð-mundsson revoked the order that Basques could be killed on sight in the region. "It is no longer legal to kill Basques in Iceland" he said. "Of course it's more for fun; there are laws in this country which prohibit the killing of Basques," Jónas said. When asked whether he's noticed an increase of Basque tourists since the order was revoked, he responded, "at least it's safe for them to come here now."

The speeches were followed by musical performances and a moment of prayer. And the inscription in memory of the Basque whalers massacred in 1615 was unveiled showing Jón lærði's words carved in stone for the future generations:

> In memory of the 31 Basque sailors massacred in 1615, "those whose ships were wrecked in a fjord close to Trékyllisvík because of the ice and bad weather in the night before St. Matthew's Mass, on September 21st, and after that they were slain by the armed men of landowner Ari Magnússon from [Ögur], while five of them were on the island of Æðey, thirteen in Sandeyri, and some time earlier, some men from two other boats belonging to the same ship were killed in the fjord of Dýrafjörður, except for one that is supposed to have escaped alive. [...] May those who are willing listen to my story, and those that do not care for it may freely leave it be."
>
> (Jón lærði Guðmundsson)

CHAPTER ONE

Basque Whale Hunting and Cod Fishery in the North Atlantic in the 16th-18th Centuries

Alvaro Aragón Ruano
Alberto Angulo Morales
University of the Basque Country

The Basque whale hunting and cod fishery in the North Atlantic is a topic covered by a certain mysterious and epic halo, which has been object of legendary and misleading interpretations, both referring to its beginning and end. The research about it come marked by State framework, as it happens with other topics related to the Basque history. Researchers used to applied modern state boundaries to the Basque Country, though Pyrenean frontiers were not definitively set until nineteenth century. This has been a major problem, since Basque economy during the Early Modern Ages has been divided into two different areas, applying an erroneous contemporary perspective: the Spanish Basque Country and the French Basque Country. However, during the aforementioned period, the Pyrenees more than a wall meant a bridge, connecting people, business and economies.

1. Basques in Newfoundland

The Basque presence in Newfoundland dates back 1517, but only in the 1530s can be considered a serious occupation, when they settled down in Placentia Bay, carrying out a significant cod fishery.[1] The Basques fisheries emerge during the second half of the sixteenth century, switching the European fishing grounds for those of Newfoundland, due to the enormous wealth of Canadian shoals and the worsening of the relationships with England, which made impossible to kept on fishing in British Islands; symptomatically, the last expedition to Ireland dated 1571. Between 1550s and 1570s important improvements happened: fishing companies turned into large-scale companies; in order to maximize investments, only largest ships were used (from 200 to 700 tons with 100 mariners and 600-1,500 Spanish barrels of 180 litres); instead of diversified companies, that were common during the 1530s and 1540s, devoted to capture both, whales and cod, a new type of specialized companies was set up (every year in Gipuzkoa about fifteen big ships were freighted for whaling and twenty five smaller ships for cod fishing). It has been calculated that between 1565 and 1577 the peninsular Basque whaling fleet expanded from 18 to 30 ships and oil cargos rose from 4,200 to 6,000 tons. Every year a minimum average of 15,000-19,000 barrels of whale oil were produced by Basques in the Strait of Belle Isle (from 6,000 to 9,000 barrels from Red Bay and another 8,000 or 9,000 barrels from St. Modeste, Chateau Bay, and other harbours) and at least 300 whales, which mean an average from 12 to 20 whales per ship, were captured; from 1530 to 1610 between 25,000 to 40,000 whales were caught.[2]

---

1   Shelma Huxley Barkham, Los vascos en el marco del Atlántico Norte. Siglos XVI y XVII (Donostia: Etor, 1987), 30. Brad Loewen and Vincent Delmas, "The Basques in the Gulf of St. Lawrence and Adjacents shores", Canadian Journal of Archaology, 36 (2012), 357.

2   Xabier Alberdi Lonbide, Conflictos de intereses en la economía marítima guipuzcoana. Siglos XVI-XVIII (Bilbao: UPV, 2012), 277-279. Loewen, "The Basques", 362. Shelma Huxley Barkham, "The Basque Whaling Establishments in Labrador 1536-1632. A Summary", Arctic 37, 4 (December 1984), 518. Álex Aguilar, Álex, "Old Basque Whaling and its Effects on the Right Whales

Most researchers state that during the final decades of sixteenth century the Basque Newfoundland's fisheries suffered serious difficulties. Different factors are claimed: cooling climate, overhunting, Native intimidation (Inuits), declining profits, the Burgos's insurers bankruptcy in 1572 or the defeat of the Spanish Armada in 1588. However, the main reason was the foreign policy of Spanish Crown in the north of Europe, which directly and indirectly damaged Basque fisheries: ships lost during wartime or as a result of piracy, markets and transport networks closed, crews and mariners confiscated in order to serve under the Spanish Navy. Foreign competition was also huge, since English, Dutch and Normans contracted Basque whalers and harpooners in order to learn how to hunt and, finally, they sent their own ships; besides, whaling was a duty of strong companies, against who the small Basque companies were suppose to be not able to compete with. But, according to Proulx, voyages to Newfoundland felt abruptly in 1579, from 30 per year to 13 for all 1580s. The main reason of this was the English Parliament act of February 1579, which closed English ports to Spanish oil: England had became the first market for Spanish oil and consequently from 1566 to 1577 the imports had risen from 200 to 2,000 tons, meaning the third of all cargos. Due to that, from 1578 to 1585 Peninsular Basques stopped hunting there.[3]

However, during the end of the century continental Basque fishers went on their expeditions to Newfoundland, mainly searching for cod, with the same structure, based on small companies. For its part, peninsular Basque fishing companies kept working thanks to insurers support, firstly from Burgos and then from Bilbo, Donostia, Vitoria-Gasteiz and inland capitals. This was mainly thanks to the proclamation of some protective measures, promoted by shipowners, investors and Gipuzkoan institutions, trying to avoid the foreign competition -principally from Lapurdi (continental

---

(Eubalena glacialis) of the North Atlantic", in Report of International Whaling Commission, (Special Issue) 10 (1986), 191-199.

3   Loewen, "The Basques", 362-363. Alberdi, Conflictos, 278. Jean Pierre Proulx, "Basque Whaling in Labrador: An Historical Overview", in The Underwater Archaeology of Red Bay: Basque Shipbuilding and Whaling in the sixteenth Century, eds. Robert Grenier, Willis Stevens and Marc-André Bernier, Vol. 1 (Ontario-Ottawa: Parks Canada, 2007), 34.

Basque coast, including Baiona)- and the pressure of the Spanish Royal Navy. However, during this period deep transformations were happening. In 1584, during the General Assembly of Zumaia, Orio complained about the progressive competition of more than 50 big ships from Donibane-Lohitzune and Ziburu, which unload in Donostia, Castro Urdiales and Bilbo their captures of cod and whale oil from Newfoundland, which was worth 140,000 ducats. Because of the petition of sailors and mariners from the Spanish Crown, fishing Gipuzkoan investments and crews moved progressively to Lapurdian expeditions. In 1582 a Royal decree authorized peninsular Basque whalers for Newfoundland that the quarter of crews were from Lapurdi and, through the petition of Getaria, another Royal decree banned in 1585 the boarding of peninsular Basque mariners in continental Basque ships. However, bans were not fulfilled, and both parts of the Basque Country kept on sharing investments and crews during the seventeenth century, though the conflicts diminished as Navy's pressure ceased. Finally, a Royal decree of 1587 ordered peninsular Basque ships to go to Newfoundland well armed and in fleet.[4]

The decrease of captures in Newfoundland forced the whale hunters to search for other grounds, such as Brazil and the Arctic, or to intensify whaling in the Bay of Biscay. Although, the Basque whaling expeditions to Brazil dated back to 1602, it was not an alternative to Newfoundland fisheries. In May 1609 two ships, owned by Lapurdian merchant Adame de Chibau, set sail from Pasaia in direction of Brazil. The expedition, which was funded by a company compound by Adame de Chibau, Julian de Breo, Julian Miguel and Pedro de Urrecha, all of them from Bilbo, returned to Pasaia in 1610 with holds full of oil.[5] Finally, in 1610, under accusation of timber smuggling, Basque activity in Brazil was banned and inhabitants of Bahia and Rio do Janeiro monopolized the whaling, using techniques learned from Basques.[6] For its part, from the end of the sixteenth

---

4   Alberdi, Conflictos, 279-284.
5   General Archives of Gipuzkoa, CO MCI 1104.
6   Thierry du Pasquier, Les baleiniers basques (Paris: Éditions S.P.M., 2000), 49-50. Priotti, Jean Philippe, Bilbao y sus mercaderes en el siglo XVI. Génesis de un crecimiento (Bilbao: Diputación Foral de Bizkaia, 2005), 187-189. Dauril Alden, "Yankee Sperm Whalers in Brazilian Waters, and the Decline of the

century it happened a revival of whaling expeditions to Galicia and Asturias from ports such as Deba, Getaria, Zarautz and Orio, during the summer.[7] Chibau was heavily involved in shipowning -supplying ships to Newfoundland- and the import of cod to Bilbo and Donostia. Firstly, associated with Diego Pereira, a prominent Portuguese merchant resident in both cities, and, therefore, by his own risk with no less than seven ships.

Chibau provided part of the approximately 10,000 ducats needed to supply the ships. In 1612, Juan Ochoa de Legorburu, a notary of Bilbo, declared that he had been drawing up such adventures for about thirty years.[8] These continental Basque shipowners were able to borrow money from their own region and from Bordeaux and La Rochelle, using it in the biggest ports of the Bay of Biscay. In the 1600s, some merchants of Vitoria-Gasteiz, Burgos and Segovia began to invest in the fish market,[9] whereas other shipowners from Donibane-Lohitzune had a close relationship with twenty merchants of Vitoria-Gasteiz between 1610 and 1614. During this five-year period, those merchants invested about 55,000 ducats in the captain Sabat de Yturbide's project, owner of a fleet of ten ships.[10] Although the inland cod and fish market in the north of Spain is not very well known, we are beginning to discern the scale of this business. From the middle of the sixteenth century, in Alcalá de Henares (Madrid), three Basque partners set up a fish company, being in force between 1569 and 1593. Antonio Alvarez de Zamudio, manager of Cenete's Marquis, Martin Pérez de Bengolea, a shipowner from Lekeitio, and

Postuguese Whale Fishery (1773-1801)", The Americas, Vol. 20, 3 (1964), 269-272.

7   Álvaro Aragón Ruano and Xabier Alberdi Lonbide, Entre Allepunta y Mollarri: Historia de un pueblo maritime (Zarautz: Zarautzko Udala, 2004), 18-21 and "«...lleben... las colas a las varrigas de los bufos...»: balleneros guipuzcoanos en las «matanzas» de ballenas en Galicia y Asturias durante los siglos XVI y XVII", Obradoiro de Historia Moderna 15 (2006), 77–111.

8   Michael Barkham, "French Basque New Found Land Entrepreneurs and the Import of Codfish and Whale Oil to Northern Spain, c. 1580 to c. 1620: The Case of Adam de Chibau, Burgess of Saint-Jean-de-Luz and Sieur de St. Julien", Newfoundland and Labrador Studies, 10 (1994), 12.

9   Barkham, "French Basque", 18.

10   Alberto Angulo Morales, "Arrantza-merkatuan Gasteizko merkatariek izandako partaidetza eta inbertsioak (XVII. mendearen hasieran)", Uztaro, 28 (1999), 37-58.

Domingo de Necolalde, a Gipuzkoan merchant, invested about 2,000 ducats. The high profit obtained from the Spanish fishing business during the first half of the seventeenth century attracted several Flemish, Italian, Portuguese and Basque merchants. Martín de Aramayona, Julián González de Trocóniz, Iñigo de Padura, Martín de Elguea or Antonio de Zavala, merchants of Vitoria-Gasteiz, kept throughout the first half of the seventeenth century an active role, running as trustees and representatives of foreign companies.[11]

2. The Basque expeditions to the Arctic

More successful were the expeditions to Iceland and Norway. Most whalers left the Belle Isle Gulf between 1612 and 1620 in favour of Spitsbergen and the north of Norway, where herds were more abundant and journey shorter.[12] Although it is not very reliable, in 1608 three Basque ships were supposed to came to Strandir, starting whaling from there. Being the whale hunting in Newfoundland's Granbaia exhausted and assuming it would be more abundant in Greenland, in 1612 Martin Argarate departed from Donostia. In one month he reached the northern coast, at 78'5 degrees north, where there was abundance of whales and commodity to hunt them. The campaign was so successful that other inhabitants of Donostia tried it. As a result, in April 1613 twelve ships departed separately from Donostia. Being there, they came across with two English privateers of 300 tons, perfectly armed. English privateers caught them, stole all their tools, supplies and captures -obliging them to go on hunting-, and, finally, sold them in Bilbao. Gipuzkoan whalers could not defend themselves, because they were not armed and they did not sail in fleet. They demanded losses estimated up at to 150,000-200,000 ducats. Responding to the appeal of Donostia's Council, the General Assembly, meet in Arrasate, designated the captain Joan de Erauso as agent of the Gipuzkoan government

---

11   María Dolores Lacabe Amorena, "Una empresa vasca de venta de pescado en el siglo XVI", Zainak, 30 (2010), 394-395.
12   Loewen, "The Basques", 376.

at the Spanish Court, in order to plead with the King about the damages received by Gipuzkoan ships during the whale hunting in Norway in 1613. Erauso took advantage of his Basque connections at the Spanish Crown, dealing with Juan de Idiaquez and the secretary Joan de Ciriza, in whose hands was the file. In March 1614 Juan de Idiaquez informed him about the probable successful end of the matter, but he regretted the delay, "...being impossible to guarantee the campaign of this year". The Gipuzkoan Government and the Council of Donostia argued that English could not claim those grounds as own land, since it was a desert and uninhabited place, 500 leagues far from England. They requested the Crown to assist them in order to go on with the campaign during 1614: on the one hand, they asked for the compensation and the end of the attacks, above all during peacetime, and, on the other hand, to help economically the whalers for the campaign. On his hand, the freighters and owners sent a report to the Spanish King requesting political actions in order to prevent English and Dutch whalers to hunt whales massively, to ban the importation of foreign bubblers, or, at least, to guarantee the preference of the local bubblers.[13]

In 1615, Argarate run at the service of the Danish King in the fisheries carried out in the north of Norway. In particular, he and other mariners from Donostia, were working in a ship of Danish King, who was trying to explode the wealth of lands recently incorporated to his crown -as a consequence of Kalmar war (1611-1613)-, firstly, hiring the Basque whalers' services and, later, expelling them from his grounds. That year, the Basques caught 17 whales and the next year 26 ships set out, though only 10 reached Iceland, being the others scattered or robbed by the English. Most of the peninsular ships spent the summer in Steingrímsfjörður and a few French ones a little farther north along the coast. At the General Assembly at Þingvellir in June 1615 a letter from the Danish King was read stating that the Spanish and others that plunder in Iceland should be captured and harmed. That summer 16 ships were in Strandir and whalers caught 11 large whales, but in September, while the ships

---

13   Municipal Archive of Hernani, E, 6, 1, 3. AGG-GAO, R 16 and JD IM 2/12/25. Alberdi Lonbide, 2012, 286-288.

were preparing to sail off, three of them broke all in Reykjafjörður. Danish caught two ships from Donostia -some merchants, such as Domingo de Galarraga, Francisco González de Legarda, Antonio de Maturana and Diego de Aberasturi, from Vitoria-Gasteiz, or Gaspar de Arriola, from Elgoibar, invested in one of the ships, called *San Pedro*, owned by captains Juan de Gayangos and San Juan del Puy, from Donostia- in North Cape or Nordkapp (Norway), 71 degrees north and 4 degrees and 39 minutes from the Arctic Circle: crews were condemned to death and ships confiscated with its supplies by Danish Treasury. Gipuzkoan Council claimed the Spanish Crown and this ordered Diego Sarmiento de Acuña, Spanish ambassador in London, to intercede with English Queen, sister of Christian IV of Denmark. Although Danish King complained about Gipuzkoan attitude, because his privileges were damaged, finally, condemned were absolved, liberated and ships returned. At that time, Basque whalers suffered similar attacks in Greenland, Iceland, Spitsbergen or Svalbard.[14]

During the seventeenth century, expeditions to the Arctic went on, but the attacks and offenses were barely repeated. In 1626 continental Basque whalers caught 20 whales and from 1656 to 1701 French are mentioned at least in fifteen occasions; the Basque presence was so continuous that a pidgin language remained.[15] This linguistic exchange, which lead to the emergence of different Basque-Icelandic glossaries, is another prove of the presence of Basques from both sides in the Icelandic shores during the seventeenth century, since the Basque words used had a remarkable dialectal diversity and origin: Biscayan, Gipuzkoan, Upper Navarrese, and Lapurdian.[16] The international context changed, taking into account that Spain and England begun a peaceful period since 1604 and Denmark was defeated in 1626 and exhausted after Thirty Years' War. Moreover,

---

14   AGG-GAO, CO MCI 1104. Pasquier, Les baleniers, 50-65.
15   Ragnar Edvardsson and Magnús Rafnsson, Basque Whaling Around Iceland. Archaeological Investigation in Strákatangi, Steingrímsfjöour, (Bolungarvík, Náttúrustofa Vestfjarða, & Hólmavík: Strandagaldur, 2006), 5-10.
16   Ricardo Etxepare & Viola Miglio, "A Fourth Basque-Icelandic Glossary", in Basque Whaling in Iceland in the XVII Century: Legal Organization, Cultural Exchange & Conflicts, eds. Xabier irujo & Viola G. Miglio (Barandiaran Chair of Basque Studies & Strandagaldu, 2015), 304.

peninsular and continental Basque whalers, in order to avoid attacks, introduced some revolutionary changes: they combined the installations of ovens on board and the sailing on fleet, paying attention to the aforementioned Royal decree of 1587. Although François Soupite, from Ziburu, is considered the inventor of the smelting system on board in 1635, Xabier Alberdi Lonbide points out that the system was being used previously by Basques, probably in order to take advantage of the sperm whales, called *trompa*, they found during the route, far from land, setting up factory vessel system.

The hunting of sperm whales was other of new sources put in practice by Basques to face the difficulties; in fact, this activity underwent its peak. The increase of sperm whale captures and its strengthening during the second half of the seventeenth century promoted the definitive setting up of sperm refining industry in Baiona, Ziburu and Donibane-Lohitzune, almost exclusively until eighteenth century. Sperm businessmen of Lapurdi interweaved a network of agents along peninsular Basque ports in order to acquire the major number of sperm whales and prevent them from competitors. At the beginning of the eighteenth century a refinery was set up in Donostia. The main market of Basque sperm -destined to the making of perfumes, cosmetics, pharmacy and even candles- was Holland and its trade did not give up during the conflicts happened along the seventeenth and the beginning of the eighteenth centuries.[17]

During the first half of the seventeenth century, it happened a geographical specialization, as a result of what Bilbo became the main port for cod imports, chiefly from British America and Norway, Donostia-Pasaia turned into the main whaling port, and Baiona into the main cod fishing port from French Newfoundland and Canada. At the same time, Basque institutions put in practice a campaign in order to obtain privileges in defence of native products. Gipuzkoan whalers petitioned the Spanish King to ban the foreign oil imports

---

17   Alberdi, Conflictos, 292-294 and "El más oculto «secreto»: las cacerías de
      cachalotes y la industria del refinado de esperma en el País Vasco durante los
      siglos XVII y XVIII", Boletin de la Real Sociedad Bascongada de Amigos
      del País, LXIX, 1-2 (2013), 331-381.

or at least to decree the preference of native oils. They were aware of the damaged that the introduction of whales hunting in England and Holland, to the date consumers of Basque oil, would caused, because it would suppose the loss of north and even Iberian markets. They were trying to avoid the free import of foreign whalebones and oil, because it would mean a price drop and the ruin of the sector.

In 1618 the crown decreed the preference of Gipuzkoan oils, forbidding the loading and unloading of foreign oils, except those from Lapurdi, in 1625 a Royal decree authorized the free introduction of cod from everywhere, in 1636 Gipuzkoan shipowners were allowed to board mariners from Lapurdi, and in 1639, after lifting the siege of Hondarribia, the Spanish Crown gave to the Gipuzkoan whalers the privilege of not being force to serve in the Navy. In 1645, although Gipuzkoan whalers were opposed, Gipuzkoa reached the permission to import 40,000 *fanegas* of salt (63,200 bushels) from France, in order to supply, among others, the ten cod ships that used to go every year to Newfoundland. Finally, in 1653 and 1675 Spanish and French crowns consented a new *Tratado de Conversa* or *Traité de Bonne Correspondance*. Despite the Franco-Spanish War (1635-1659), from the 1640s aforementioned protective policy started working: in 1643 six ships were ready to go to Newfoundland and Norway, and in 1655 in Biscay and Gipuzkoa there were more than thirty fishing ships. During this period, the investments and the crews continued being from both sides of the frontier; two thirds of Gipuzkoan crews were from Lapurdi.[18]

However, these treaties, which protected the privileges reached by continental Basque fishermen, actually damaged the Gipuzkoan whalers. Continental Basques were allowed to introduce their oils in Gipuzkoa and, for that, they had the support of merchants from Donostia, who did not matter about the origin or nationality of oil, but the opposition of peninsular Basque whalers. This competition caused the decrease of Gipuzkoan fleet, from 18 in 1655 to 13 ships in 1669. This year, shipowners of Donostia petitioned the preference of their oils, before those of continental Basques. In order to fight the monopoly practiced by Bilbo, Gipuzkoan authorities encour-

---

18   Alberdi, Conflictos, 295-309.

aged the preparation of continental Basque cod expeditions from Pasaia. But, new difficulties came to whaling. Joint to the foreign competition and the reduction of captures, forcing whalers to reach further northern places, during 1680s wars and political instability increased. As a result, Gipuzkoan fleet dropped: in 1681 there were 8 whalers and 4 cod fishers, which became 2 in 1695. Moreover, in 1696 and 1697 Louis XIV banned continental Basques from boarding in Gipuzkoan whaling ships and Guipuzkoans from hunting in Newfoundland's French settlements, instead of being agreed a new *Traité de Bonne Correspondance* in 1695. Nevertheless, that year 9 whaling ships fished in the Arctic. Finally, the banning expired and in 1698 one cod ship and in 1699 two went to Newfoundland.[19]

As previously has been stated, Basques did not left Newfoundland, though most of expeditions were related to cod fishing. Period from 1630 to 1713 was the apogee of Basque cod fishing and the good understanding between peninsular and continental Basque whalers and fishers. The appetite for cod fishing flourished in the three Basque maritime lands and ships from three of them came to Placentia, which became French capital of Newfoundland in 1662, mainly during the first half of the seventeenth century: 20-30 Lapurdian ships and 30-40 Gipuzkoan ships. From 1630 to 1713, Lapurdian fishing crews frequented the Gulf's southern littoral, while Gipuzkoans and Biscayans made the northeast (*Gran Baya*) their favoured destination;[20] for instance, in 1669 Pedro de Odria wrote a letter to Luis de Veroiz asking him 50 barrels of *Grambaya* in order to sell them in Castile, because it had good sales during the winter, due to «it did not freeze, as a result of its nature, just the opposite that happens with Sarda (right whale)».

Basques from all three provinces continued to congregate at Placentia Bay, in harmony with French authorities. In order to avoid the difficulties, at the end of the seventeenth century, they used a common strategy: they sailed under command of Lapurdian captains and French flag. According to the testimonies of a proof carried out in 1697, peninsular Basque cod fishers had been using

---

19   Alberdi, Conflictos, 317-327.
20   Loewen, "The Basques", 378-383.

this strategy for at least fifty six years, that is, from about 1640, in order to fish cod in Newfoundland's ports.[21]

Fortunately, we have some accounts of whalers (*La Esperanza* and the previously aforementioned *San José*) and cod fishers (*San Pedro*) of Donostia from 1675 to 1678. These ships sailed from the middle of April until the middle of September from Pasaia, under French flag -they paid the passport to the Lord of Semper (Senpere), Governor of Baiona. Freights varied from about 42,000 to 70,000 *reales de plata* and did so the captures, from 188 to 683 barrels. For instance, the more expensive was that of *San José*, which was worth 70,143 *reales de plata*: 28,864 *reales* for common supplies, 30,000 *reales* for about 900 barrels and 10,509 for salaries under a bottomry contract (25 per cent). However, the most complete was that of the *San José* in 1676. The crew was formed of 50 mariners, including the surgeon, whose origin was diverse: 13 from Orio, 10 from Getaria, 3 from Deba, 2 from Elantxobe (Biscay), 10 from Donostia and 11 "French", from Hendaye. The freight cost 54,341 *reales de plata* (including supplies, salaries and the bottomry) and the *average* (i.e. costs and taxes in the port) 1,917 *reales de plata*, meaning a total cost of 56,258 *reales de plata*, whereas profits amounted to 143,430 *reales de plata*, taking into account that a barrel was worth 14 *pesos* (i.e. 210 *reales de plata*). In the case of Roman Ramery, the principal investor, who shared the half of the freight investing about 27,170 *reales de plata*, his profits amounted to 49,770 *reales de plata*. Therefore, in this campaign -not all of the campaigns were as successful- Ramery earned 22,605 *reales de plata*, almost the double of the invested money.[22]

21   General Archives of Gipuzkoa, SS 329 and 330.
22   General Archives of Gipuzkoa, SS 329 and 330.

3. Towards the end of Basque fisheries in the North Atlantic Sea

During the eighteenth century, three were the main problems for the Basque fisheries. Firstly, the development of British Colonies' fisheries replaced the European fishers, above all from the 1720s, when new techniques were put in practice, cutting prices and costs of cod fishing. Thus, products from British and French Colonies in North America gradually replaced European products. Due to that, progressively, instead of fishing in Newfoundland, Biscayan and Gipuzkoan fishers formed trade expeditions, supplying French and English colonies with European and Spanish equipment and domestic goods in exchange of their cod; this system, called *trocada* or in exchange, replaced little by little the direct fishing. Secondly, from the middle of the seventeenth century Dutch oils fled the European markets. Thirdly, the exhaustion of whales in northern hemisphere was causing the reduction of captures and forcing hunters to go to northernmost grounds, being more difficult to gain good captures. For instance, the average of captures by Dutch fleet in the 1730s was from 2'6 to 3'8 whales, whereas among Lapurdians the average dropped from 7-8 to 3 between 1725 and 1737. Due to that, from the beginning of the eighteenth century whalers made up for all their losses going to other grounds, such as Galicia and Ireland, and increasing sperm whales' captures. Fourthly, it was increasingly difficult to preserve the protective legislation, since it was an obstacle for the complete development of the import of foreign fishing products, desired by merchants of Donostia. Taking advantage of the critical political situation at the beginning of the eighteenth century (Spanish Succession War and Treaty of Utrecht) the aforementioned laws definitively came to an end. In 1708 a Royal decree established the freedom to import foreign fishing products and the end of the preference for native oils.[23]

---

23   Pasquier, Les baleniers, 214-220. Loewen, "The Basques", 388.

While Gipuzkoan institutions had a clear commitment with commerce, marginalising the whaling industry, they were trying to restore the cod fishing in Newfoundland, claiming for their historical rights, in an attempt to avoid the monopoly of Bilbo. In the meantime, as it happened during the seventeenth century, along the first decades of eighteenth century Basque fishers of both sides of the frontier, but mainly the peninsular Basques, thanks to the *Traités de Bonne Correspondance*, used in their ships false passports or neighbouring letters, pretending to be owned by continental Basques, in order to avoid attacks from Turkish and Berber pirates, traditional allies of France. Before finishing the Spanish Succession War, in 1712, Donostia claimed to Gipuzkoan institutions to demand in the peace negotiations the fishing freedom in Newfoundland, fearing that England was going to eliminate it. As a result of Utrecht Treaty in 1713, France was expelled from Hudson, Acadia and Newfoundland, though they kept its fishing rights. The loss of Newfoundland in 1713 moved French interests and fisheries toward Cape Breton Island, known as Île Royale, being Louisbourg the government centre.[24] In the case of Gipuzkoans, through the 15th article of the Treaty, England went along with their fishing rights, whether they proved their historical rights; however, it was impossible, since there was no title or Royal decree. Later in 1717 the Marquis of Monteleon, Spanish ambassador in London, claimed that before being under English sovereign, there were some treaties between Spain and France -thanks to what Spanish fishers were allowed to fish in French grounds-, which were recognized, so the Spanish rights to fish in French ground were in force.[25] Along the eighteenth century, there were several more attempts, but none of them succeeded and Spanish ships were captured (1721, 1748, 1752, 1761 and 1781).[26]

In particular, in 1758 the English privateers *St George* and *Europe* caught and bring to Bristol and Falmouth four ships sailing from Donostia and Bilbo to Newfoundland, with liquor in exchange for

24   Loewen, "The Basques", 384.
25   Margarita Serna Vallejo, Los viajes pesquero-comerciales de guipuzcoanos y vizcaínos a Terranova (1530-1808): regimen jurídico (Madrid: Marcial Pons, 2010), 158-163.
26   General Archives of Simancas, Estado, 7014. Alberdi, Conflictos, 350-366.

cod, under French flag: the *San Ignacio de Loyola*, owned by Juan Ignacio de Cardón and captained by Juan Bautista de Ecenarro, the *San Lorenzo*, owned by Ignacio de Goicoechea and commanded by Jorge de Urtategui, both from Donostia, the *San José*, captained by Martin de Uribe, and the *San Joaquín*, leaded by captain Francisco de Iturralde, from Bilbo. The case of *San Ignacio de Loyola*, built up in Baiona as *St Esprit*, is very expressive. It was loaded with flour, liquor and salt, in order to dispatch it to the French settlements of Newfoundland, as the cargo and supercargo declared before the Court of Baiona's Admiralty, but later it was fraudulently sold to the aforementioned Juan Baustista Ecenarro and carried to Pasaia with the captain and twelve mariners, from where departed to Louisbourg. On his part, Juan Enrique Goossens, the freighter, Thomás Sant Aulari, owner of the *Santo Tomás*, and Luis Violet, owner of the *La Villa de Bilbao* and *El Gran San Luis*, merchants of Bilbo, requested the return of the ships caught by English when they travelled to Newfoundland with Spanish flag and crew, and Spanish King's passport.[27]

Juan Enrique Goossens, was agent of the Big Maritime Insurance Company of Paris in Bilbo, founded in 1750 by, among others, his brother *Pedro Francisco Goossens* y Mazo (Bilbao, 1701-1775), who was born in a Dutch family settled in Bilbao and, after moving to Paris around 1732, became French naturalised in 1743. This cosmopolitan businessman, before the Seven Years War (1756-1763), drew up a project to trade with Russia, trying to break the Anglo-Dutch tobacco monopoly. He also set up a company with a Louisbourg merchant settled in La Rochelle, for the purpose of fishing and trading cod and other fishing products in French North America and sell them in France and the West Indies.[28] Goossens returned to his homeland in 1762, being appointed to the Spanish Treasury Board Minister and General Treasurer in 1766.[29]

---

27   General Archives of Simancas, Estado, 6944-3 and 6.

28   Jean François Bosher, "Financing the French Navy in the Seven Yars War: Beaujon, Goossens et Compagnie in 1759", in Business in the Age of Reason, eds. R.P.T. Davenport-Hines, Jonathan Liebenau (London: Frank Cass, 1987), 121.

29   Román Basurto Larrañaga, "Linajes y fortunas mercantiles de Bilbao del siglo XVIII", Itsas Memoria, 4 (2003), 348.

The fish trade to Bilbo from Denmark, Sweden, Norway and Iceland went on during the first half of the eighteenth century, but it declined in the second half. The business community of Bilbo spent several years trying to open trade routes with Buenos Aires and other colonial places. The first attempt to develop the Goossens' projects began in Madrid in 1763[30] and continued in Bilbo in 1764, trying to set up a trading company for Louisiana -under Spanish control-, created with a capital of 600,000 *pesos*. In exchange for this project, his partners requested the exploitation of snuff and cod there.[31] French ships (from Baiona and Donibane-Lohitzune) and several ports of New England, New Brunswick, Nova Scotia and Canada carried out the fish trade from Newfoundland and other North Sea's grounds to Bilbo. The flagship product was the cod: every year hundred thousand quintals arrived in Bilbo in the mid-eighteenth century and arrivals had a growth of fifty per cent by the end of the century.[32]

During the negotiations carried out by the Spanish ambassador in London, Count of Fuentes, in 1760 Pitt blurted him out, visibly annoyed, "...this is an issue that English never would admitted, being improbable the Spanish right and privative the English right: this is my verdict and I would rather cease as minister than accepted it; but, in case of cessation, I would do it".[33] The Treaty of Paris (1763) definitively finished this controversy: the 18th categorically stipulated that the Spanish King desisted, as well for himself as for his successors, from all pretension which he may have formed in favour of the Gipuzkoans, and other his subjects, to the right of fishing in the neighbourhood of the island of Newfoundland. However, the 5th article proclaimed the liberty of fishing -renewing the 13th article of the Treaty of Utrecht-, on condition that the subjects of France do not exercise it but at the distance of three leagues far from any

---

30   Pilar León Tello, Un siglo de fomento español (años 1725-1825): expedientes conservados en el Archivo Histórico Español (Madrid: Ministerio de Cultura, 1980), 128.

31   Teófilo Guiard y Larrauri, Historia del Consulado de Bilbao, Vol. 2, (Bilbao: La Gran Enciclopedia Vasca, 1972), 72.

32   Guiard, Historia del Consulado, 394.

33   General Archives of Simancas, Estado, 6949-7 and 9; 6943-22, 24 and 32; 6944-2.

English possession in the Gulf of St. Lawrence and fifteen from Cape Breton, and the 6th that French fishers could settled in St. Pierre and Miquelon, in order to carry out their fishing. Therefore, continental Basques could keep going to Newfoundland.[34]

This mainly affected the cod fisheries, but no the whaling, taking into account that whales hunting had already moved to other grounds: in 1718, there were six whaling ships in Donostia: *San Vicente, Santiago, San Francisco, San Joseph, Santa Theresa* and *Jesus, Maria & Joseph*. In this field, however, new difficulties appeared during the eighteenth century. In 1717 the exemption from the Spanish Navy, enjoyed by peninsular Basque fishers from 1639, was definitively removed. Due to that, it became common for the peninsular Basque fishers to board in continental Basque ships: in 1730 a third of Lapurdian crews in cod fishing and whaling ships were peninsular Basques, and from 1730 to 1733, in the apogee of whaling Lapurdian industry, 65 per cent of crews-members were peninsular Basques. Apart from the need of workforce, Lapurdians boarded peninsular Basques because they had not to pay taxes for their part of the captures. Despite the fact that this changed in 1722, when Donostia started to demand some taxes on all barrels, during the 1720s and the 1730s Gipuz-koan fishers massively boarded (from 100 to 200 mariners) the 20 Lapurdian whaling ships (there were just two Gipuzkoan whaling ships) that were spending the winter in Pasaia -which property was shared by some peninsular Basques, such as Aragorri, Mirubia or Del Cerro. But when in 1728 the Royal Company of Caracas set up, the competition around mariners arose and exploded into a deep controversy between Gipuzkoan institutions and the majority of merchants of Donostia facing the whalers and whaling investors. Comparing with mariners of the Royal Company of Caracas or the Royal Navy, whalers earned higher salaries.[35]

In order to avoid this, the Royal Company of Caracas put in practice diverse strategies: in 1729 a Royal decree imposed the Navy Enrolment; boarding in Lapurdian whaling ships was repeatedly

---

34   http://avalon.law.yale.edu/18th_century/paris763.asp [consulted the 2nd of January 2015].
35   Alberdi, Conflictos, 366-389.

banned; and, in order to compensate the losses happened in the Battle of Cape Passaro (1718), where the six whaling ships were destroyed, in 1732 was set up the Whaling Company of Donostia, which in 1733 had three ships and gained the protective privileges not long ago removed. From 1740 to 1748, during the Austrian Succession War, they did not work and for 1749 just one of those ships operated: it had a poor campaign in Davis Strait. In 1753 the Royal Company of Caracas absorbed the company and tried to make it operative setting up two ships, but the results were chaotic and it was definitively liquidated in 1761. Besides, the conjuncture turned into favourable for the Royal Company: from the 1730s the Lapurdian fleet dropped (in 1737 in Pasaia spent the winter just 8 ships and in 1751 just 4, owned by the Whaling Company of Baiona, in force between 1749 and 1755), because of the progress of big English and Dutch fishing companies, against which nothing could be done. Once it was clear that the ships of Royal Company had enough crew, the rest of mariners were allowed to boarded Lapurdian ships. Moreover, in 1742 Spain and Denmark reached a commercial agreement, establishing the commercial freedom between both countries, except for Spanish America and the northern Danish possessions: Iceland, Faroe Islands, Greenland, Norland and Finnmark. That was not very favourable for whaling interests, but the final thrust was the rupture of diplomatic relationships in 1753 and the declaration of war in 1756. In its part, before the Seven Years War (1756-1763), in 1755 England conquest French Acadia causing the decline of Whaling Company of Baiona and Lapurdians fisheries, which finished in 1758. However, some Lapurdians were reported fishing in 1767 in St. Pierre, Port-au-Choix or Ferrolle.[36]

Finally, Southern replaced the North Atlantic, and Antarctic and Patagonia the Arctic and Newfoundland. The *Reflexiones sobre el comercio español a Indias,* written by Campomanes in 1762, included two chapters dealing with the convenience of promoting Spanish fisheries in America. Campomanes estimated that half a million

---

36   Lauriel Turgeon, Pêches basques en Atlantique Nord (XVIIe-XVIIIe siècle). Etude d'economie maritime (Burdeos: Université de Bordeaux, 1982), 260. Pasquier, Les baleniers, 263-266. Alberdi, Conflictos, 399-410. Loewen, "The Basques", 384.

quintals of cod were imported by the British merchants, representing an annual loss of two million pesos for Spain.[37] The project aimed to set up factories for whale and sea-wolf hunting in Patagonia (Bahía de San Julián and Puerto Deseado). In 1775 was founded the General Company of Maritime Fishing, in order to recover the whaling activity, to put in practice the Enlightenment' ideas, such as those of Campomanes, and to fulfil the desires of the Spanish Crown to control the Southern Atlantic and Patagonia. Two of the main promoters were José Ventura de Aranalde, a merchant of Donostia, commissioner for the oil sale of the Portuguese Company, and Antonio Sáñez Reguart, who in 1789 agree with the possibility to setting up the whales and seals hunting there, causing the foundation of the Royal Maritime Company. Despite the royal support and the good results harvested in the first campaign, the Company never got over the debt incurred at the beginning. During the Revolutionary Wars and the French occupation of Donostia between 1794 and 1795, the Company was not working, but the colonies founded by it were in force until 1807.[38]

---

37   Carlos Martínez-Shaw, "Las reflexiones de Campomanes sobre la pesca en América", Chronica Nova, 22 (1995), 248.
38   Alberdi, Conflictos, 410-416. Serna, Los viajes, 49-51. María Teresa Luiz and Monika Schillat, Monika, La frontera austral. Tierra del Fuego 1520-1920 (Cádiz: Servicio de publicaciones de la Universidad de Cádiz, 1997), 51. María Ángeles Faya Díaz, "Jovellanos y la pesca: iniciativas para su fomento en el norte de España", in Jovellanos, el valor de la razón (1811-2011), coord. Ignacio Fernández Sarasola et al. (Oviedo: Instituto Feijoo de estudios del siglo XVIII, 2011), 453-464.

Table 1. Annual consumption of Bristish Codfish in Spain during 1770

Port	Population	English Fish (quintals)
Barcelona	92,000	57,000
Valencia	100,000	10,000
Denia		9,000
Alicante	17,000	50,000
Cartagena	60,000	15,000
Almeria		4,000
Malaga	42,000	14,000
Cadiz	70,000	110,000
Ferrol		20,00
Vigo	6,000	
Corunna		
Gijon	6,000	
Santander	2,000	
Bilbo	12,000	90,000
Donostia	9,000	2,000
Canary & Balearic Islands		5,000
Other Ports		20,000
TOTAL		406,000

Source: James G. Lydon, Fish and Flour for Gold, 1600-1800
(Philadelphia: Library Company of Philadelphia, 2008), 67.

Why these projects emerged in the mid-eighteenth century? An anonymous document from the National Historical Archive in Madrid, entitled *Observations on the British Fisheries*,[39] allows us to offer an approximate image of the business struggle in order to control the fisheries of northern Europe and America. This text explains the phenomenon of promoting British fisheries since 1745. Within this report, the whale hunting is described as a matter of

---

39   National Historical Archive, Estado, 3188/425.

great importance and utility, but, at the same time, like a "really lottery game", which needed a big capitalization. Dutch were who, provided by better trade and financial organization's tools, became the master of Greenland's whaling. The report concluded recommending the British authorities a better fish market regulation, an improvement of the fishing funding and the professionalization of the activity. On his hand, in a report carried out in 1787 about the profits achieved by Great Britain before 1776 from Newfoundland, this land was considered the "British Peruvian mine", due to the profits going back every year, which worth 579,548 £. It was calculated that 27,710 British people spent the summer in Newfoundland (22,200 men, 1,510 women and 4,000 children) and 15,000 stayed there during the winter. Every year 763 ships (43,541 tons), 2,650 boats (18,550 tons) and 250 shallops or launches (2,500 tons) arrived in Newfoundland.[40] This British foreign policy,[41] against which Jovellanos and Bilbo traders warned, went hand in hand with the decline of Dutch fisheries power.[42]

Table 2. Annual British profits in Newfoundland before 1776 (1787)

Good	Weight	Price	British £
Codfish	754,310 quintals	13 £ / quintal	409,301
Cod liver oil	3,046 tons	13 £ / ton	48,736
Marinating salmon	2,400 "tierces"	45 s / tierce	5,400
Sea lion oil	1,050 tons	16 £ / ton	16,800
Skins			2,400
Juniper			15,000
Sea lion skin			910
TOTAL			579,548

Source: General Archives of Simancas, Estado, 8145, 25.

---

40   General Archives of Simancas, Estado, 8145, 25.
41   David J. Starkey, Jon Th. Thor & Ingo Heidbrink, Ingo, eds. A History of the North Atlantic Fisheries. Volume 1: From Early Times to the Mid-Nineteenth Century (Bremerhaven: German Maritime Museum, 2008).
42   Charles Ralph Boxer, "The Dutch Economic Decline", in The Economic Decline of Empires, ed. Carlo Cipolla (New York: Routledge, 2006), 243.

4. Conclusions

Whereas, during the sixteenth century, Basque whale hunters and cod fishers choose Newfoundland and the Atlantic Coast of Canada, from the beginning of the seventeenth century, they moved to the northern countries: from Norway, Iceland or Greenland to the Spitsbergen, Svalbard or Hudson and Davis Straits. Newfoundland kept on being the main destiny for cod fisheries until the beginning or the eighteenth century, though sporadic hunting of whales and seals was never given up. Artic whale expeditions lasted until the 1760s, when new tries were done in the Southern Atlantic, chiefly in the coast of Patagonia. Differ from coastal fishing, transoceanic expeditions had a capitalist organization, where ship owners set up companies sharing agreements with other investors, infrastructure owners or crews, subscribed insurances or buying and selling contracts of victuals and supplies necessary for expeditions and of products of captures. Into this network not only was involved the coast, but also the inland, linking places as far away as Segovia and Donostia. Therefore, during the Early Modern Ages, Basques (peninsular and continental Basques) led the way to the industrial fishing, though their apprentice (English, Dutch and Danish) had finally to marginalize them.

References

Alberdi Lonbide, Xabier. Conflictos de intereses en la economía marítima guipuzcoana. Siglos XVI-XVIII, Bilbao: UPV, 2012.

_____"El más oculto «secreto»: las cacerías de cachalotes y la industria del refinado de esperma en el País Vasco durante los siglos XVII y XVIII", *Boletin de la Real Sociedad Bascongada de Amigos del País* LXIX, 1-2 (2013): 331-381.

Alden, Dauril. "Yankee Sperm Whalers in Brazilian Waters, and the Decline of the Postuguese Whale Fishery (1773-1801)", *The Americas* Vol. 20, 3 (1964): 267-288.

Aguilar, Álex. "Old Basque Whaling and its Effects on the Right Whales (Eubalena glacialis) of the North Atlantic", *Report of International Whaling Commission* (Special Issue) 10 (1986): 191-199.

Angulo Morales, Alberto. "Arrantza-merkatuan Gasteizko merkatariek izandako partaidetza eta inbertsioak (XVII. mendearen hasieran)", *Uztaro* 28 (1999): 37-58.

Aragón Ruano, Álvaro and Alberdi Lonbide, Xabier. Entre Allepunta y Mollarri: Historia de un pueblo maritimo, Zarautz: Zarautzko Udala, 2004.

_____ "«...lleben... las colas a las varrigas de los bufos...»: balleneros guipuzcoanos en las «matanzas» de ballenas en Galicia y Asturias durante los siglos XVI y XVII", Obradoiro de Historia Moderna 15 (2006): 77–111.

Barkham Michael. "French Basque New Found Land Entrepreneurs and the Import of Codfish and Whale Oil to Northern Spain, c. 1580 to c. 1620: The Case of Adam de Chibau, Burgess of Saint-Jean-de-Luz and Sieur de St. Julien", Newfoundland and Labrador Studies, 10 (1994): 1-43.

Barkham, Michael. "La industria pesquera en el País Vasco peninsular al principio de la Edad Moderna: ¿una edad de oro?", Itsas Memoria, 3 (2000): 29-75.

Basurto Larrañaga, Román. "Linajes y fortunas mercantiles de Bilbao del siglo XVIII", Itsas Memoria, 4 (2000): 343-356.

Bosher, Jean François. "Financing the French Navy in the Seven Yars War: Beaujon, Goossens et Compagnie in 1759", in Business in the Age of Reason, edited by R.P.T. Davenport-Hines & Jonathan Liebenau, 115-133. London. Frank Cass, 1987.

Boxer, Charles Ralph. "The Dutch Economic Decline", in Carlo Cipolla (ed.), The Economic Decline of Empires, edited by Carlo
Cipolla, 235-263. New York. Routledge, 2006.

Edvardsson, Ragnar and Magnús Rafnsson. Basque Whaling Around
Iceland. Archaeological Investigation in Strákatangi, Steingrímsfjöour. Bolungarvík: Náttúrustofa Vestfjarða, & Hólmavík: Strandagaldur, 2006.

Faya Díaz, Mª Ángeles. "Jovellanos y la pesca: iniciativas para su
fomento en el norte de España" in Jovellanos, el valor de la
razón (1811-2011), coordinated by Ignacio Fernández Sarasola
et al., 453-464. Oviedo. Instituto Feijoo de estudios del siglo
XVIII, 2011.

Guiard y Larrauri, Teófilo. Historia del Consulado de Bilbao, Vol. 2,
Bilbao: La Gran Enciclopedia Vasca, 1972.

Huxley Barkham, Shelma. "The Basque Whaling Establishments in
Labrador 1536-1632. A Summary", Arctic 37, 4 (December
1984): 515-519.

____Los vascos en el marco del Atlántico Norte. Siglos XVI y XVII,
Donostia: Etor, 1987.

Lacabe Amorena, Mª Dolores. "Una empresa vasca de venta de pescado en el siglo XVI", Zainak 30 (2010): 392-420.

León Tello, Pilar. Un siglo de fomento español (años 1725-1825): expedientes conservados en el Archivo Histórico Español. Madrid:
Ministerio de Cultura, 1980.

Loewen, Brad and Delmas, Vincent. "The Basques in the Gulf of St.
Lawrence and Adjacents shores", Canadian Journal of Archaology 36 (2012): 351-404.

Luiz, María Teresa and Schillat, Monika. La frontera austral. Tierra
del Fuego 1520-1920. Cádiz: Servicio de publicaciones de la
Universidad de Cádiz, 1997.

Lydon, James G. Fish and Flour for Gold, 1600-1800. Philadelphia:
Library Company of Philadelphia, 2008.

Martínez-Shaw, Carlos. "Las reflexiones de Campomanes sobre la pesca en América", Chronica Nova, 22 (1995): 243-267.

Pasquier, Thierry du. Les baleiniers basques. Paris, Éditions S.P.M., 2000.

Priotti, Jean Philippe. Bilbao y sus mercaderes en el siglo XVI. Génesis de un crecimiento, Bilbao, Diputación Foral de Bizkaia, 2005.

Proulx, Jean Pierre. "Basque Whaling in Labrador: An Historical Overview", in The Underwater Archaeology of Red Bay: Basque Shipbuilding and Whaling in the sixteenth Century, edited by Robert Grenier, Willis Stevens and Marc-André Bernier, Vol. 1, 25-96. Ontario-Ottawa, Parks Canada, 2007.

Turgeon, Lauriel. Pêches basques en Atlantique Nord (XVIIe-XVIIIe siècle). Etude d'economie maritime. Burdeos: Université de Bordeaux, 1982.

Serna Vallejo, Margarita. Los viajes pesquero-comerciales de guipuzcoanos y vizcaínos a Terrnaova (1530-1808): regimen jurídico. Madrid: Marcial Pons, 2010.

Starkey, David J., Thor, Jon Th. and Heidbrink, Ingo, eds. A History of the North Atlantic Fisheries. Volume 1: From Early Times to the Mid-Nineteenth Century. Bremerhaven: German Maritime Museum, 2008.

CHAPTER TWO

The Ubiquitous Basque Mariners

William A. Douglass

> "The English were preceded in the whale fishery
> by the Hollanders, Zealanders, and Danes..."
>
> *Moby Dick*, Herman Melville

Arguably, Melville's *Moby Dick*, first published in 1851, is the iconic fictional treatment of whaling within world literature. The book, however, presumes to be more than a novel since it interweaves a history and ethnography of the industry among the chapters that advance the story line. The author conducted serious library research regarding the past and simply got it wrong, because at no point does he take into consideration the Basques. Indeed, he tells us,

Perhaps the only formal whaing code athorized
by legislative enactment, was that of Holland. It
was decreed by the States-General in A. D. 1695
But though no other nation has ever had any
written whaling law, yet the American fishermen
have been their own legislators in this matter.[43]

There is an extensive literature regarding Basque maritime activities
from the early Middle Ages down to the present. Denizens of the
Cantabrian seacoast, Basques have been depicted as Europe's earliest
whalers. Many of the coastal villages have images of cetaceans on
their escutcheons and regulations regarding whaling (including the
division of the spoils) date from as early as the late twelfth along the
Basque coast.[44] Some claim that Columbus learned of a landmass
across the Atlantic (he believed it to be the Orient) from Basque
whalers or cod fishermen active off its shores.[45] What is certain is
that by the early 1500s, or two centuries before Melville's Dutch
baseline, Basque whalers and cod fishermen maintained seasonal
land operations during summers in Newfoundland to process their
catch before returning to their homeland in the autumn.[46] Many of
the papers in this conference deal with the brief presence here in
Iceland of Basque whalers in the early sixteenth century, including
fascinating cultural exchanges, including formulation of primitive
Basque-Icelandic dictionaries, and a truly tragic chapter in the Icelandic sagas—the slaughter of a number of Basque whalers in 1615.[47]

---

43   Herman Melville, *Moby Dick* (New York: Penguin Books, 1992), 432.

44   Mariano Ciriquiain-Gaiztarro *Los vascos en la pesca de la ballena*, San
Sebastián/Donostia: Biblioteca Vascongada de los Amigos del País, 1961,
131-140.

45   William A. Douglass and Jon Bilbao, *Amerikanuak: Basques in the New
World* (Reno: University of Nevada Press, 1975), 53-55.

46   Margarita Serna Vallejo, *Los viajes pesquero-comerciales de guipuzcoanos
y vizcaínos a Terranova (1530-1808): régimen jurídico* (Madrid, Barcelona,
Buenos Aires: Marcial Pons, 2010).

47   Ragnar Edvardsson and Magnús Rafnsson, Baque Whaling Around
Iceland. Archeological Investigation in Strákantangi, Steingrímsfjörður,
Reykjavik: Náttúrustofa Vestfjarda Fornleifaeild, 2006.

Yet the Basques were more than skilled and adventuresome fishermen. They were the consummate mariners of the kingdom of Castilla. By the thirteenth century, Basque vessels plied the trade routes of both the European Atlantic littoral and the Mediterranean. In the fourteenth century they maintained a "House of Bizkaia" in Bruges to facilitate their North Atlantic trade and were negotiating commercial treaties with England. In the service of both the Portuguese and Castilian crowns they participated in the exploration of North African waters and the equatorial African Atlantic beyond. Antonio de Nebrija, a contemporary of Christopher Columbus, stated: "Those who resided in the County of Bizkaia and the province of Gipuzkoa are people wise in the art of navigation and forceful in naval battles, and they have ships and appurtenances for them, and in these three regards they are better informed than any other nation of the world."[48] Indeed, some of Columbus's vessels were constructed in the Basque Country and and a significant part of the crews of his four voyages to the New World were Basques. Beatriz Enríquez de Arana, the admiral's mistress and mother of his son Hernando, was part Basque and some of her brothers served Columbus.

Basque maritime technological innovations were fundamental in the development of the vessels that facilitated long-range probes of the planet's vast oceans. Regarding the defining vessel of the epoch's transoceanic exploration, French historian Pierre Chaunu noted, "The oldest caravels appeared in the Gulf of Biscay: from 40 to 50 tons and with two square sails. There is evidence [of them] as early as the thirteenth century. This ship, transformed progressively, was used by Henry the Navigator." Referring to the mid-1400s, Australian historian O.H.K. Spate observed,

---

48   Quoted in José Ignacio Tellechea Idígoras »hHistorias de la mar, » in *Itxasoa : El mar de Euskalerria. La naturaleza, el hombre y su historia,* ed. Enrique Ayerbe, vol. 2 (Donostia/San Sebastián : Eusko Kultur Eragintza Etor), 1988), 249. Quoted in Miguel Laburu, "Jalones en la historia de la arquitectura naval vasca," in *Itxasoa, El mar de Euskalerria. La naturaleza, el hombre y su historia,* ed. Enrique Ayerbe, vol. 2 (Donostia/San Sebastián : Eusko Kultur Eragintza Etor, 1988), 222.

Shipbuilding underwent a virtual revo-
lution in the fifteenth

century.... Iberian builders, particularly those of Biscay, played an

important role in this development, without which the Discoveries

would not have been possible....
Thus, from about 1430 a

bewildering variety of hybrids
[ships] were developed, initially it

seems largely by the Basques.... The
end result, the standard big ship

for most of the sixteenth century, was the carrack: three masts with

a lateen mizzen, high castles (especially aft), and a large central

cargo hatch. This was the *nao* of the
Spanish *Carrera* and *nau* of the

Portuguese *Carreira* to the West
and East Indies respectively.[49]

Famously, Pope Alexander VI divided the world between Spain
and Portugal in 1494 to alleviate competition between the two Iberian bearers of the sword and the cross. At that time, it remained
impossible to calculate longitude and there was no clear idea of the
circumference of the globe. The so-called Tordesillas Line was meant
to recognize Portuguese African and Asian exploratory initiatives
while conferring most of the Americas to Spain. In point of fact, it
resolved little, including the immediate status of the coveted Spice
Islands, since both Iberian powers concluded that they fell within
its orbit. Their Tordesillas Treaty did, however, establish that the

---

49   O.H.K. Spate, *The Spanish Lake* (Canberra: Australian National University,
       1979), 16.

world's largest body of water, the Pacific Ocean, was what Spate would come to denote the "Spanish Lake" in his history of Pacific exploration.

I have just published a book entitled *Basque Explorers of the Pacific*[50] which analyzes their activities both as notable personages and as an Iberian ethnic group within the ranks of the many expeditions sent by Spanish monarchs and Latin American viceroys into Pacific waters. I have been requested to discuss some of its features in this talk. I believe that this is the first monograph to view through a Basque ethnic lens the two and a half centuries of Spanish exploration of the entire region from the Pacific coast of the Americas to the Philippines, and Spice Islands, as well as China and Japan, and from the two Californias and northwest coast to the elusive fabled land of *Terra Australis*, or Australia.

Within three decades of Columbus's first voyage, Charles V dispatched Ferdinand Magellan in search of a southern passage around the South American continent as the key to a westerly route to the East Indies (1519) and Hernan Cortés was probing northward from the Pacific coast of Nueva España (1522) in quest of fabled fortune and a sea route to the Orient, including a possible northern passage that would shorten considerably the distance between Europe and East Asia. They were stories of incredible perseverance against overwhelming odds. Fueled by a combination of Christian zeal and treasure-seeking cupidity. Magellan was, of course, Portuguese and while some regard him to be the first to have circumnavigated the globe, he was killed in the Philippines. It would be the Gipuzkoan Basque, Juan Sebastián de Elkano, who straggled into San Lúcar de Barrameda on September 6, 1522, almost three years to the day after the expedition's departure from that port, accompanied by 18 other European survivors and four Spice Islanders. Elkano was received by his monarch and accorded many honors, including the right (emblazoned upon his family escutcheon) to claim to have been the first circumnavigator. To be sure, he is extolled to this day in the Basque Country as a hero of the first order. Thanks to

---

50   William A. Douglass, *Basque Explorers of the Pacific* (Reno: Center for Basque Studies, 2015).

his involvement, there were many other Basques recruited for the Magellan expedition. However, there was a dark side to the man as well. In 1519 he was a fugitive from Spanish justice. During the voyage itself Elkano joined others in a mutiny off the South American coast against their admiral. Elkano received a death sentence that was commuted only because the expedition needed every available hand.

In the wake of the first circumnavigation, the Spanish monarch moved quickly to send a second expedition under the command of García Jofre de Loaísa to further establish a westerly route to the Spice Islands. Given his experience, Elkano was appointed second in command. Four of the expeditions sseven vessels were constructed in Basque shipyards and Elkano recruited many Basques for them, including several of his own relatives and a page, Andrés de Urdaneta, who was dedtined for greatness in his own right. After an extremely difficult traversal of the Strait of Magellan, Loaísa succumbed to scurvy at the outset of the Pacific crossing. Elkano assumed command, but died himself a few days later, surrounded entirely be his Basque inner circle (including Urdaneta) to whom he commended part of his inheritance.

Meanwhile, in Nueva España, in 1532 Cortes dispatched two ships under the command of Diego Hurtado de Mendoza to explore the Pacific coastline coastline in search of the fabled Strait of Anián, or northern passage, and to assert the viceroy's claim to any discovered lands along the way. They disappeared and so the following year Cortés dispatched two more vessels to look for them—one under the command of his cousin, Diego de Becerra. Becerra's pilot was the Basque Fortun Ximénez de Bertadona. In the event, he and several other Bizkaians mutinied and killed Becerra in his sleep. The mutineers then landed on the southern tip of Baja California near the present-day port of La Paz—becoming the first Europeans to set foot in the Californias. They did not survive to tell the tale since they were in turn killed by Indians.[51]

Urdaneta spent eight years in the East Indie before returning to Spain in 1535. By then he had travelled extensively throughout

---

51   *Ibid.*, 122.

the Spice Islands and spoke several of the local language. He was also a keen student of the region's winds and currents. In 1540 he relocated to Nueva España where twelve years later in 1552 his life would take a new twist. He became an Augustinian cenobite in Mexico City. In the event, his withdrawal from the world was interrupted when the Spanish monarch and Nueva España's viceroy decided to launch a new probe of the Pacific. They ordered the friar's superior to make him available as the obvious person to organize the expedition. Urdaneta recruited his friend and fellow Basque Miguel López de Legazpi to oversee the initiative, harboring the hope that they would explore the unknown southern seas in search of the elusive southern continent--but it was not to be. By this time the Spain had relinquished any claim on the Spice Islands to Portugal; consequently, the Spanish authorities wanted to colonize the Philippines as their foothold in the Orient. The obedient friar's official position would be leader of the expedition's contingent of Augustinian missionaries. De facto, however, he would be its experienced navigator. It took five years to prepare the expedition and that set sail from La Navidad on June 1, 1564.

Urdaneta remained but a few months in the Philippines, assisting Legazpi in the implementation of what would prove to be the most enlightened and humane native policy in Spanish colonial history. There remained a major challenge, however, that of discovering a dependable return route to Nueva España. The journey from the Americas to the Philippines was facilitated by prevailing winds in the middle latitudes, but it was their existence that inhibited any return voyage. There had been several Spanish attempts to sail from the Spice Islands to the New World by this time—all failures. Urdaneta's earlier observations of the currents and seasonal shifts in the wind patterns of insular southeastern Asia had convinced him that if one sailed to the north at the proper time of the year there would be seasonal easterlies. In June 1, 1565, left the Philippines on a vessel nominally commanded by Legazpi's sixteen-year-old grandson Felipe de Salcedo. There was a large contingent of Basques on board and Urdaneta provided the real navigational expertise. It took them months to complete the longest human sea voyage to date, no less than 11, 160 miles, before reaching the California coast. And thus was established the famed Manila Run that for nearly two centuries exchanged New World silver for Oriental, and particularly Chinese, goods.[52]Subsequently, Basques would play a prominent role, indeed key, in the exploration and mapping of the California coastline, as well as that of the Pacific northwest as far as north as Alaska. Fabled explorers of northern Pacific waters such as Sebastián de Vizcaíno, Bruno de Hezeta y Dudagoitia, Juan Francisco de la Bodega y Quadra, and Juan Manuel de Ayala y Aguirre were all Basques, and my book, recounts the exploits of each.

I would conclude this hagiography by describing my favorite protagonist in Pacific exploration—Pedro Sarmiento de Gamboa. Son of a Galician father and Bizkaian mother, his birthplace is unknown as are details of his early years. His real biography begins in Peru where he settled after a sojourn in Mexico. In both colonies he fell afoul of the Spanish Inquisition for impiety and necromancy. In 1565 he was tried and convicted in Lima and ordered to do public penance for his sins before being banished from the New World. During his stay in Peru, Sarmiento had collected Inca legends that convinced him of the existence of both an elusive El Dorado to the east of the Andes and a fabled land in the southwestern Pacific that might even host Solomon's lost mines. There remained interest in the quest for the southern continent as well, and Peru's viceroy organized an expedition in search of it. Given his problems on land, Sarmiento was quick to enroll in this ultramarine adventure, insisting that he had been its inspiration and that he should be named its commander.

Nevertheless, to Sarmiento's chagrin, not only did the viceroy appoint his young and inexperienced nephew, Álvaro de Mendaña, as the 1567 expedition's admiral, Mendaña in turn passed over Sarmiento in choosing his navigator. Furthermore, Mendaña was a pious man more in search of souls and peaceful coexistence with native peoples than of fortune. The two men would quarrel frequently and, when the expedition made land in the Guadacanal area, Sarmiento regularly overstepped the bounds of his authority.

---

52   *Ibid.*, 103-137.

He kidnapped a chief, looted a village of all of its foodstuffs, and killed several natives in revenge for their lethal attack on a Spanish landing party. In desperate straits, Medaña polled his men regarding their next move. Sarmiento stated brashly that he feared no native and urged that they continue their search for treasure and the southern continent.

Instead, Mendaña ordered that the expedition's two ships set sail for California. By this time, Sarmiento was pointedly no longer on board the flagship and the two vessels became separated at sea by a storm. Both made it to Nueva España after an arduous three-month crossing and were reunited in Colima and their longstanding animosity now became a feud. Mendaña seized all of Sarmiento's papers and charts while Sarmiento formally accused his admiral of dereliction of duty. When Mendaña rejoined the viceroy in Peru, Sarmiento remained behind in Central America, fearing that he might be imprisoned by Mendaña's uncle.

It was then Sarmiento's good fortune to meet Don Francisco de Toledo in Panama. Toledo was on his way to Peru to assume his new post there as Mendaña's uncle's replacement as viceroy. Toledo was duly impressed with Sarmiento and named him his chief cosmographer and chronicler. In this role Sarmiento accompanied the new viceroy on a five-year visitation throughout the realm. Along the way he gathered oral histories from elderly surviving Inca leaders and penned the first history of Peru in which he justified Spanish conquest of the Incas on the grounds that they too had been conquerors of other Andean peoples and usurpers of their lands. Sarmiento also participated in the siege of Vilcamba, last redoubt of the Incas, and claimed to have personally captured the rebellious Tupac Amaru.

In 1575 was again arrested and imprisoned by the Spanish Inquisition for necromancy. In 1578 he was convicted anew but was released from prison after he agreed to recant and do public penance. He avoided banishment from Peru only through Toledo's intervention. Nevertheless, his destinies with fate were far from over. The following year the corsair Francis Drake rounded Tierra del Fuego and wreaked havoc up the South American coast. When he entered the harbor of Callao, Toledo and the officials of the Peruvian audiencia dispatched two vessels to pursue the audacious Englishmen. Sarmiento was convinced (correctly) that the corsair was headed for Nueva España and recommended trying to intercept him there. However, the viceroy's son insisted they go to Panama so he could continue on to Spain to report to the royal authorities. Drake managed to escape and then disappeared altogether before turning up back in London having become the second circumnavigator of the globe.

Meanwhile, Peruvian authorities feared that Drake might be headed back to Europe via southern South America. They dispatched Sarmiento to the Strait of Magellan. He entered it from the Pacific and traverse its length, becoming the first European to have done so. He proceeded to Portugal where he met with Spanish King Philip II, Portugal's newly installed monarch as well. Sarmiento gave a glowing account of the abundant wild game, moderate climate and agricultural potential of the Strait. He was therefore charged with establishing agricultural settlements there and with fortifying them against future English and other potential European intruders into the Spanish Lake.

Thus began another sad chapter in Sarmiento's history. He recruited more than five hundred colonists for his venture, including many Basques. Basques were also numerous and prominent in the ranks of his ships' officers. However, this initiative was incorporated by King Philip into the more ambitious plan of creating an Armada of the South Seas (no fewer than 23 ships and 3,000 participants) to secure the Pacific Coast of the Americas and protect the Manila galleons. Once again Sarmiento was placed under a feckless supreme commander—Diego Flores de Valdés. He shared this fate with Alonso de Sotomayor, governor of Chile, and commander of 600 troops.

Thanks to Flores's dithering, the convoy left Spain after the proper sailing time and was immediately decimated by an Atlantic storm, losing six ships and eight hundred men. It then sailed to Brazil where it was decided to winter over. By the time the expedition headed south, Sarmiento and Flores were no longer on speaking terms. At the Rio de la Plata, Sotomayor abandoned the ill-fated venture and marched his men across the pampas and over the Andes to Chile. When Flores and Sarmiento reached the strait their first two attempts to enter it were thwarted and Flores ordered the fleet back to Brazil. Flores then departed South America with the main force, leaving behind five ships under the command of Diego de Ribera and 548 intending colonists under Sarmiento's authority. On February 1, 1583, they were again at the mouth of the Strait of Magellan.

Sarmiento managed to establish two colonies in Tierra del Fuego after a major loss of supplies in a shipwreck, hostile attacks by Indians, and mutinies in both settlements. Diego de Ribera abandoned the mission and Sarmiento's flagship ship was later swept out to sea by a storm. It took him and his crew 34 day to reach Brazil during which they experienced extreme cold and were reduced to chewing on leather for their only sustenance.

Sarmiento found some supplies in Rio that Diego de Ribera had left behind before sailing off for Europe, and he dispatched them aboard a rescue vessel (in the event, it failed to reach the colony). Sarmiento then headed south with more provisions on a different boat and was shipwrecked, surviving only by paddling ashore on two boards that were nailed together. He organized yet another rescue mission that was in turn thwarted by a major storm. By now more than two years had passed since he was blown out of the Strait of Magellan and Sarmiento decided to sail to Spain in search of assistance for the colonists.

Near the Azores his caravel was seized by English privateers in the service of Sir Walter Raleigh. Sarmiento arrived in Plymouth as a captive on August 31, 1586. But in no time he had became a friend and confidant of his captor. Sarmiento and Raleigh conversed in Latin and the Englishman was entranced by Sarmiento's book of South American history, and particularly its description of El Dorado to be found somewhere in Guyana. The year was 1586 and there were strained relations between England and Spain. After an interview with Queen Elizabeth arranged by Raleigh, Sarmiento was released and was quite possibly serving as messenger for Elizabeth on a secret diplomatic mission to King Philip when he was apprehended in southern France and imprisoned by the Count of Bearn, the future King Henri IV. During the four years that Sarmiento languished in prison Philip launched the ill-fated Spanish Armada (1588) against England—many of its vessels were constructed in Basque shipyards and then manned by Basque officers and mariners.

In 1590, Sarmiento was finally ransomed by Philip and proceeded to the Spanish court where he pleaded for assistance for his South American colony, initially totally unaware that by then both had perished. Perhaps fittingly, the ultimate demise of this controversial man is itself shrouded in mystery. Some believe he died in Portugal or aboard a ship plying the Atlantic to the New World. Others have surmised that he was the "Pedro Sarmiento" who died in the South Sea while commanding an abortive assault from the Philippines upon Tidore in the Spice Islands.[53] Samuel Eliot Morison summed up Sarmiento's career with the words, "No more truehearted, loyal, and brave man ever sailed the far-off seas."[54]

I conclude the book on an ironical, even humorous, note. The Basques have often been called "the mystery people of Europe" largely based upon the uniqueness of their language and their genetic differences from other Europeans, particularly as reflected in the serological evidence. In 199 Australian writer Robert Langdon published a book entitled *The Lost Caravel* followed in by its sequel *The Lost Caravel Revisited*. Langdon was trying to account for the observations of some European explorers of some peoples in the South Pacific with European features, on the one hand, and the more recent evidence that Basques and certain groups in western Polynesia have similar (and the world's highest) incidences of key genetic markers.

Langdon speculates that the donors were Basque mariners aboard the *San Lesmes*, a vessel that was separated from the rest of Loaísa's fleet upon entering the Pacific from the Strait of Magellan and then disappeared without a trace. In Langdon's view, it likely made it to

---

53   *Ibid.*, 138-161.
54   Samuel Eliot Morison, *The European Discovery of America*, vol. 2, *The Southern Voyages, A.D. 1492-1616* (New York: Oxford University Press, 1974), 707.

Polynesia where the survivors disseminated their genes, making their descendants "the mystery people of the Pacific."[55] Delicious!

55   Douglas, *Basque* Explorers, 227-230.

CHAPTER THREE

Baskavígin:
The Massacre of Basque Whalers

Tapio Koivukari
Xabier Irujo

The incident in the autumn at 1615 on West fiords of Iceland, known as *Baskavígin* or the Slaying of the Basques, is documented most thoroughly in Jón Guðmundsson's writing *The true story of the shipwreck and killing of the Spaniards* or *Sönn frásaga af spanskra manna skipbrotum og slagi*.[56] In his older years Jón wrote also an autobio-

---

56 Although some authors have made reference to this historic event as "Spánverjavígin" or the slaying of the Spaniards, Guðmundsson did not coin the term "Spánverjavígin" and he never used it. In fact, the term was not used until the late nineteenth century, and not as a compound word, but as a phrase: "Víg spánverjanna." The first to use this phrase was Ólafur Davidsson in 1895 in an article entitled "Víg Spánverja to Vestfjörðum 1615 og Spönsku Visur eptir síra OLAF Söndum" published in the journal Tímarit Hins íslenzka bókmentafélags (vol. 16, pp 88-163). Before other terms such as "dráp" and "aftaka" were used. When Jónas Kristjánsson published the first academic edition frásaga Sonn in 1950 he entitled it "Spánverjavígin 1615", and was published in Copenhagen by Hið íslenzka fræðafélag. The

graphical poem called *Fjölmóður*, 'the sanderling', a bird with which he identified, in which he narrated again the events that took place in 1615. Jón Guðmundsson *the Learned* (or 'the Wise', lærði in Icelandic) was a self-educated man, a paracelsianist and Renaissance man, but an Icelandic commonman who lived betwee 1574 and 1658 without many possibilities for higher education.

In order to write *Sönn frásaga* Guðmundsson interviewed some of the persons who had directly taken part in the events that he narrated. Among them was Rev. Jón Grímsson, pastor at the Árnes parish[57] in Trékyllisvík, and five of his closest neighbours all of whom participated in the massacre, which "is why they could bring home such news and tell us how things had developed as will be explained here."[58] Guðmundsson himself witnessed some of the events he relates, such as the arrival of the whalers and the hunting season off the Strandir coasts in the summer of 1615 and indicated that he will "represent these events and occurrences as they reported them."[59]

The methods used in the writing of *Sönn frásaga* place Jón Guðmundsson's report as an early example of modern journalism that predates the first deontological codes of journalism by various centuries.[60] Guðmundsson reports true events in an objective way by contrasting and comparing various sources of information while looking for all available sources of information. He filtered the collected information, trying to report what he believes to be trustworthy information, regardless of how uncomfortable that may be for anyone involved, including himself. The author further

---

expression became then popular in Iceland. However, some years later Jónas Kristjánsson participated in the congress organized by Ólafur J. Engilbertsson at Snæfjallaströnd in 2006. Kristjánsson entitled his article "Baskavígin" and it was published under this title in the proceedings of the congress. We have adopted the term Baskavígin given to the massacre by Jónas Kristjánsson in 2006.

57   Jónsson, Már, "Introduction". In Irujo, Xabier and Hólmfríður Matthíasdóttir (Eds.), *1615: Spánverjavígin / Euskal baleazaleen hilketa / La matanza de los vascos / The slaying of the Basques*, Forlagið, Reykjavík, 2015, p. 166.

58   Irujo, Xabier; Matthíasdóttir, Hólmfríður (Eds.), *1615: Baskavígin / Euskal baleazaleen sarraskia / La masacre de los balleneros vascos / The Massacre of Basque Whalers*, Euskal Erria, Montevideo, 2015, p. 261.

59   Ibid.

60   *Statements of Principles* of the American Society of News Editors, http://asne. org (retrieved June 18, 2015).

refused to accept any personal benefits for his journalistic activity and reports what he believes to be the truth even when it could be used against him and, most important, he wrote his report immediately after the events occurred.[61]

Moreover, Guðmundsson proved to be open to different and partly unknown cultures and behaviors, different ways of thinking and, stood up to those that manipulated the information in order to generate hatred based in prejudices and misinform the general public. His ethics code is embodied in the lapidary statement at the end of the Preface to his report: "May those who wish to listen to my story do so, and those that do not care for it may freely leave it be."[62]

Based on his work ethics and the quality of his writings, *Sönn frásaga* represents a remarkable source of historical information, undoubtedly the most relevant one in order to shed light on the events that took place in 1615.

Apart from *Sönn frásaga* , the massacre is also mentioned in two poems, the anonymous narrative poem *Víkinga rímur*[63] 'Viking stanzas', written close to Patreksfjörður, where the mariners that survived the massacre spent the winter and, the *Spænsku vísur*, or 'Spanish Stanzas', composed by Rev. Ólafur Jónsson (ca. 1560-1627), pastor at Sandar, is a second example of anti-whaler propaganda.[64] As Magnús Rafnsson states, the authors of these two poems link the events that took place in Strandir to the aggressive behavior of the Basque whalers. Pictured as criminals, they threatened the local inhabitants and carried out serious crimes. Ari Magnússon, on the

61 Villanueva, Ernesto, *Deontología informativa. Códigos deontológicos de la prensa escrita del mundo*, Porrúa, México, 2002, p. 21.

62 Irujo, Xabier; Matthíasdóttir, Hólmfríður (Eds.), *1615: Baskavígin / Euskal baleazaleen sarraskia / La masacre de los balleneros vascos / The Massacre of Basque Whalers*, Euskal Erria, Montevideo, 2015, p. 262.

63 *Víkinga rímur*, in Kristjánsson, Jónas, *Spánverjavígin 1615. Sönn frásaga eftir Jón Guðmundsson lærða og Víkinga rímur*, Möller, Copenhagen, 1950, pp. 29-76.

64 The significance of the Spanish Stanzas is essentially historical, and for that reason we included it in its first English translation in Irujo, Xabier; Miglio, Viola (Eds.), *Basque Whaling in Iceland in the 17th Century: Legal Organization, Cultural Exchange and Conflicts*, University of California, Santa Barbara/Barandiaran Chair of Basque Studies and Strandagaldur, 2015, pp. 109-138.

other hand, is pictured as the noble, heroic leader of Westfjords.[65] Further, the 1615 massacre is also mentioned in Icelandic annals and the court decisions, both from Súðavík before the later slayings and then from the Mýrar in the January 1616 and Holt in the summer 1616.

Iceland at the time of the events

The population of Iceland was around 50.000 inhabitants.[66] People were farmers or peasants, but due to the climate they were not growing crops. The main living on agriculture was sheep and cattle herding. Farms were on the average very small and 90 percent of the Icelandic peasants were tenants. The land was owned by the crown and the church and the richest peasant families. There were no noblemen or aristocracy on Iceland, but a small minority, the peasant elite, owned and controlled the land and also manned the positions of government and church with its own sons. A lot of land properties belonged to the crown and to the church and was thereby controlled by the clergymen and magistrates, same persons who belonged to the certain families.[67] Iceland was a part of the kingdom of Denmark and was ruled by the county magistrates. Big decisions were taken at the parliament or Alþingi every summer but local governors and magistrates were in control of the different districts of the country.[68]

It was difficult to marry if one did not own a farm or have a control over it as a tenant. Unmarried persons who could not stay

---

65 Rafnsson, Magnús, "Cultural Exchange and Socialization in the Westfjords", in Irujo, Xabier; Miglio, Viola (Eds.), *Basque Whaling in Iceland in the 17th Century: Legal Organization, Cultural Exchange and Conflicts*, University of California, Santa Barbara/Barandiaran Chair of Basque Studies and Strandagaldur, 2015, p. 302.

66 Karlsson, Gunnar, *The History of Iceland*, University of Minnesota Press, Minneapolis, pp. 45-51.

67 Jóhannesson, Guðni Th., *The History of Iceland*, Greenwood, Santa Barbara (Cal), 2013, pp. 43-59.

68 Pencak, William, *The Conflict of Law and Justice in the Icelandic Sagas*, Rodopi, Amsterdam, 1995, pp. 14-22.

in their parent's house had to hire themselves as farm hand or maid. Twice a year, in spring and autumn, there the "moving days" were held when it was allowed to hire to or from another farm. Thus, everyone had some place to stay, a minimum living anyway.[69] To own a boat a person was required to have a control over a farm, as an owner or a tenant. Icelanders considered themselves as farmers, not fishermen, and the ruling class wanted to keep it that way, as a consequence, people was not allowed to settle down in fishing stations and become full-time fishermen. This policy was followed both to secure the labor force for the farms and, as well, living on fishery alone on the open boats was considered very insecure. In addition, cod kept itself in deep waters, not available for ground fishing, and there was not enough wood to build better and decked boats for fishery in deep waters, nor enough wood to build barns to storage more hey for the cattle. Peasants missed some of the sheep every hard winter. Life in the country was harsh in the 17th century.

Every now and then a whale drifted ashore and was of course utilized, but it belonged to the landowner in the first place. Icelanders did not hunt whales themselves, their boats were small and they had not developed yet a technique to hunt and process "sea cows."[70] According to the customs and legends of the day, it was not advisable to say "whale" aloud, one had to use words like "the big one" or even "the cow". As pointed out by Horrebow in the 18th century, "it is commonly reported, that the noise and bellowing of these animals make the-cows ashore run mad; but none here ever saw any of these supposed animals, or noticed the bad effects of their bellowing."[71] However, when possible, whale meat was eaten and the bones were used in the construction of torf houses.

---

69 Dennis, Andrew; Foote, Peter; Perkins, Richard (Eds.), *Laws of Early Iceland: Grágás I*, Univ. of Manitoba Press, 2014.

70 Barkham, Michael M., "La industria pesquera en el País Vasco peninsular al principio de la Edad Moderna: ¿Una edad de oro", *Itsas Memoria. Revista de Estudios Marítimos del País Vasco*, 3, pp. 29–75, 2000.

71 Horrebow, Niels, *The Natural History of Iceland: Containing a Particular and Accurate Account of the Different Soils, Burning Mountains, Minerals, Vegetables, Metals, Stones, Beasts, Birds, and Fishes; Together with the Disposition, Customs, and Manner of Living of the Inhabitants*, A. Linde, 1758, p. 88.

Iceland being a part of the kingdom of Denmark was a Lutheran country. However, differences in religion does not seem to have been the main issue in the distrust and conflict between the Basque and Icelanders. The age of hard-core confessionalism had not really begun in the early 17th century. Gissur Einarsson, one of the earliest promoters of the Reformation in Iceland, served as the first Lutheran bishop of Skálholt between 1540 and 1542. It was between 1542 and 1627 that Guðbrandur Thorláksson established Lutheranism in Iceland.[72] In 1615 there were a lot of catholic survivals in Icelandic piety. For instance, Jon Guðmundsson himself thought that giving up the catholic faith was not that good idea. He wrote in his poem that in summer 1614 a Basque captain wanted to take some young people with him back to the homeland to be brought up Catholic. It has not been recorded that this ever happened. Anyway, we can assume that the difference in religion had a co-effect when suspicion between Basques and Icelanders begun to spread in the fall of 1615.

There had been four very hard winters in the beginning of the century. And again, the winter of 1615 was very hard, the polar drift ice had been lying on the shores until the end of May, preventing fishing and pasturing on the shore. The worry about the sufficiency of the food was realistic. Foreign fishermen were fishing and trading around Iceland but also privateers and corsairs had been acting in the coasts of Iceland. At 1614 an English pirate ship had been plundering for two weeks in Vestmannaeyjar, a town in the south coast of Iceland. A gang of pirates made an attempt to hijack a Danish trader in Patreksfjörður, a town located on the shores of the southern West Fjords named after Saint Patrick and, although these pirates were seized and executed, the fear of pirates might have extended to all foreign sailors.

Due to the conflicts with sailors in the coasts of Iceland, the Alþingi had sent a complaint to the King of Denmark in Copenhagen. In the spring 1615 the King sent his answer to the Icelandic parliament proclaiming that the Icelanders as well as the Dan-

---

72   Gassmann, Günther; Oldenburg, Mark W., *Historical Dictionary of Lutheranism*, The Scarecrow Press, Toronto, 2011, p. 405.

ish merchantmen had the right to defend themselves from the "Biscayans"[73] as well as from other foreigners: they were allowed to kill them and take their ships and possessions from them. The decree states "considering that during the past summer, Basque mariners and others were hunting whales in our waters around the coasts of Iceland, and that there they robbed our subjects, banished them from their own homes, and caused great damage and losses,"[74] the ships coming from "Buschaien" (Bizkaia or, generically, the Basque coast) could be attacked, and their crew murdered, without receiving any punishment for said crimes. The decree was ratified by the Icelandic parliament (Alþingi), in July 1615.[75]

Trading in Iceland became a Danish monopoly as for 1602, and the King had developed a consistent policy to preserve the loyalty to and the interests of the Danish Crown by taxing or prohibiting the inhabitants of the island to agreed contacts with other nations and merchant forces. By the law, Danish merchantmen held a monopoly in trade at a certain trading post on Iceland and they had to sail to their trading posts every summer. Therefore, no stranger was allowed to stay in Iceland over the winter.

The Reformation allowed the Danish Crown to appropriate all possessions of the Catholic Church on the island, including considerable amounts of land, which became the property of the king, but was administered by local representatives. The administrators of these expropriated lands became some of the most powerful land owners in Iceland, carrying out administrative and executive functions on behalf of the king of Denmark. Ari Magnússon of Ögur (1571-1652) was one of these magistrates or local representatives of the King in Ísafjarðardjúp and Strandir district, in the Westfjords of Iceland, in 1615. He was son of Magnús the Neat, and belonged to the powerful Svalbarð family. He was one of the most influential and

---

73   In Jón lærði's text, as in other Icelandic documents of this period, the Basque whalers are referred to as Biscayans (pars pro toto), as was common also among the Spanish authors of the time.

74   Jónsson, Már, "Introducción". In Irujo, Xabier; Matthíasdóttir, Hólmfríður (Eds.), *1615: Spánverjavígin / Euskal baleazaleen hilketa / La matanza de los vascos / The slaying of the Basques*, Forlagið, Reykjavík, 2015, p. 164.

75   Kristjánsson, Jónas, *Spánverjavígin 1615. Sönn frásaga eftir Jón Guðmundsson lærða og Víkinga rímur*, Möller, Copenhagen, 1950, p. xxv.

richest men on Iceland. Magnússon married Kristín, the daughter to Guðbrandur, bishop of Northern Iceland, thus increasing his influence by marrying outside of his circles.

First arrival of the Basque to Strandir in 1613

Jón Guðmundsson wrote that the Basque whalers came for the first time to Strandir, at the east shore of the Westfjord peninsula, by 1613. The Skarðsá annals also reported eighteen whaling ships hunting whales off the Icelandic shores in 1613. Pillaging and violence occurred in some places but the Sjávarborg annals underline the fact that the Basque whalers behaved peacefully in 1613[76], which is also corroborated by Jón Guðmundsson who got to know two of the Basque sailors, Juan and Martin Argarate (*Jóhann* and *Marteinn de Argaratte*), "who returned home without any stealing or quarrel."[77] Guðmundsson also expressed that "this is something that the people around here know, if they only cared to admit it."[78]

With seventeen captured whales, the hunting season in 1613 was excellent, due in part to the collaboration between the local population and the whalers, among whom Guðmundsson mentions "the good pastor Ólafur", Ólafur Halldórsson[79]. Halldórsson, pastor in Steingrimsfjörður, guided the Basques to Steingrimsfjörður, probably to Hveravík, where the remains of a whaling station have been excavated. Guðmundsson expressed that Ólafur had had good relationship with the Basques. Unfortunately he died before 1615. Basque whalers came back in 1614 and some quarrels were reported, but nothing serious happened.

---

76 Jónsson, Már, "Introducción". In Irujo, Xabier; Matthíasdóttir, Hólmfríður (Eds.), *1615: Spánverjavígin / Euskal baleazaleen hilketa / La matanza de los vascos / The slaying of the Basques*, Forlagið, Reykjavík, 2015, p. 161.
77 Irujo, Xabier; Matthíasdóttir, Hólmfríður (Eds.), *1615: Baskavígin / Euskal baleazaleen sarraskia / La masacre de los balleneros vascos / The Massacre of Basque Whalers*, Euskal Erria, Montevideo, 2015, p. 216.
78 Ibid.
79 Guðmundsson, Jón, *Fjölmóður*. In Huxley, Selma (Ed.), *Itsasoa. El mar de Euskalerria. La naturaleza, el hombre y su historia*, Etor, Donostia, 1987, p. 300.

In the autobiograhical poem *Fjölmóður*, Guðmundsson also added that Ari Magnússon of Ögur arrived to Kaldbaksvík in 1613 and sold the Basque a license for whaling and collecting the driftwood in Steingrímsfjörður for 600 *reales*.[80] Selling licenses was openly against the law and most probably Ari never reported to the Danish king who never received any money from the rights owed to him from this industry.

The summer of 1615

Sixteen ships came from the Basque to Iceland in 1615 but only three of them stood in. As Guðmundsson reported, at arrival the Basque whalers obtained a permit for their ships to drop anchor off the Strandir coast from Ari Magnússon who let the local population know that if more ships came, they needed to obtain a permit from him. The rest of the boats sailed for northern Norway and maybe more eastward, "to Russia", wrote Guðmundsson. There was still some ice lying on the shore when the ships arrived in the late spring and two of the boats got stuck in the ice near a place called Eyjar, close to the mountain of Bala. Icelandic fishermen at Eyjar attacked them. As Guðmundsson wrote, they wanted to kill the Basques in order to gain some fame and keep their possessions but the Basques defended themselves and nobody was killed. The leader of the Basques was a chief harpooner named Ascensio.[81]

The captains of the three ships that stayed in Iceland in 1615 were Esteban Telleria and Pedro Agirre nicknamed 'the Prudent',[82] who had sailed together earlier, and Martin de Villafranca[83] who had the biggest ship of the fleet. The three ships had a total crew of 86

---

80   Irujo, Xabier; Matthíasdóttir, Hólmfríður (Eds.), *1615: Baskavígin / Euskal baleazaleen sarraskia / La masacre de los balleneros vascos / The Massacre of Basque Whalers*, Euskal Erria, Montevideo, 2015, p. 216.

81   Guðmundsson mentions that those twelve ships went on to 'Moscoviam', that is Russia, even if it is most likely that they would have gone rather to northern Norway.

82   Pétur Agvirre, Pétur Ageirus or Pedro de Argvirre and Stefán or Stephan de Tellaria in the original writing.

83   Martinus Billa de Franca, Martinum á Frakkaþorpi, Marteinn af Frakkaborg or Martin af Frakkaborg.

men, most of them from Gipuzkoa, and specifically from the cities of Donostia and Mutriku. The ships were lying at Reykjarfjörður in Strandir, south of Trékyllisvík. They hunted and processed up to eleven whales and sold the inhabitants much inexpensive whale meat. He also says that Asunción harpooned some smaller whales for the local people, and praised him for his charity. Guðmundsson mentions that after the incident on the Eyjar the Basque whalers were very cautious and underlined that Pedro and Esteban and their men behaved themselves all well.

Guðmundsson states that the crew of the Basque ships had done no pillaging, or committed any illegal act for which they deserved punishment. According to the author, their behavior was honorable: this applied to the whole crew on Agirre's ship, and most of the crew on Telleria's ship, except for two rascals that had stolen a sheep or socks from a farm where they thought they had enemies since the Eyjar riots earlier that year. The author also says that a few men on Villafranca's ship were aggressive when they were not under the immediate supervision of their captain. Those had also taken a sheep from farms that had not agreed in selling it to them willingly. Guðmundsson also points that Villafranca had saved an Icelander's life, who had hit one of his crew members with a stone and left him unconscious and concludes, "in this way, that summer went by without any major event, thievery or swindling, apart from what was mentioned. Men from other parts also went to them every day, both on horseback and by boat, as if the whalers' ships were just another commercial town. One could get hammers, axes, iron, and burlap for sails from them. Our pastor let hardly a day go by without visiting them".[84]

The local population is also described by Guðmundsson as peaceful, living together and collaborating willingly with the foreign whalers. Later on in the autumn some blubber was stolen from a head of a whale at the whaling station.

---

84   Irujo, Xabier; Matthíasdóttir, Hólmfríður (Eds.), *1615: Baskavígin / Euskal baleazaleen sarraskia / La masacre de los balleneros vascos / The Massacre of Basque Whalers*, Euskal Erria, Montevideo, 2015, p. 267.

The farmer who lived next to the station refused to say, who had taken the blubber, and Pedro and Martin took both a sheep from him. Martin gave the man some biscuits and some *naparra* or red wine from Navarre.

Reykjarfjörður, September 1615

The three Basque captains held a meeting onboard Martin's ship on Tuesday, 19 September.[85] They made the distribution of the hunting campaign among the ships and the crew, and had a good meal and wine. Pedro and Esteban went back to their ships and Martin went with some of his men to visit Jón Grímsson, pastor of Árnes. He thought that the priest owed him for the whale meat he had bought in the summer and Martin suspected that the blubber was also stolen for the priest. Anyway, he wanted some sheep for his trip and the priest refused. Martin got angry and let his men threaten to hang him. The priest promised to give them a calf next morning. Martin and his men went back to their ship. Guðmundsson refers that "of those events I only have the pastor's version."[86]

On the night of Wednesday, September 20th, on the eve of St. Matthew's Mass, a sudden storm happened. A strong and unusual south-eastern wind broke into the fiord and the waves carried blocks of ice towards the shore, and during the night the storm caused the ice to collide repeatedly against the ships: "The drift ice closed in around both Pedro's and Esteban's ships. We were there until the evening, and went afterwards to the farm closest to that place. After sunset a most unusual and pernicious storm blew the pack ice against both ships, but a headland was also in the way with very high cliffs. The first ship to miss its moorings was Esteban's ship and it hit Pedro's ship with the drift ice and all, until everything about the helm was broken. Then it sank with all the cargo that they had

---

85 Guðmundsson follows the Julian calendar. According to the Gregorian calendar, September 19 was not Tuesday, but Saturday, and the night between September 20 and 21 was the night between Sunday and Monday.
86 Ibid.

acquired, and Pedro's ship must have been pushed by the other and produced a frightful and powerful din until it was crushed against the headland, splitting down the middle. Its aft part got stuck on a rock on the headland, so that it was possible to wade from it up to the beach, but its fore part sank into the deep. Moreover, because the ice became a solid hard sheet that evening, all the boats that were by the ships were broken to pieces".[87] Villafranca's ship was also pushed around and broken: "First the rudder was broken, then the hull was pierced through in many places so that the sea water got in."[88]

Three men died, Ascensio, 'a good man and excellent hunter', Pedro's cousin Luis and a young boy. Guðmundsson went to the site and saw these men who had lost everything in question of hours: "Those poor chaps were in such dire straits, and so crestfallen that first day, that people didn't need to go very far to find them".[89] On September 22nd, a Friday on the Julian calendar, many of the local inhabitants arrived to the area, and so did Jón Guðmundsson himself, with a certain Bjarni Ámunsson. Jón Grímsson came also with his calf but captain Villafranca did not want it any more. Agirre asked if Grímsson could write a letter of recommendation for him and his men, to keep them safe, which he did. Men discussed what they should do; Guðmundsson offered four men, including Agirre and his pilot Andreas, to stay in his house over the winter. According to Icelandic law they had to announce that they were poor and in need, and then the authorities had to look after them. However, Agirre could not accept the generous offer and abandon his men. Basque whaling campaigns were organized as cooperative enterprises, run and operated in an associative way.[90]

Grímsson suggested that they should go to Jökulfirðir, where would be a sailing ship owned by a local farmer, probably hoping they'd leave the area as soon as possible. The Pastor also suggested

87   Ibid., p. 270.
88   Ibid.
89   Ibid., p. 270.
90   Irujo, Xabier; Miglio, Viola (Eds.), *Basque Whaling in Iceland in the 17th Century: Legal Organization, Cultural Exchange and Conflicts*, Barandiaran Chair of Basque Studies – University of California, Santa Barbara, 2015, pp. 155-211.

that they should break up into smaller groups and ask for charity in various farms along the way, which the Basque mariners did. Despite Guðmundsson's advice, the Basques decided to sail with their *txalupas* over to Jökulfirðir, which includes sailing around the Horn, the northernmost point of Icelandic Westfjords.

It took some days to the whalers to recover from the shock, take a decision and prepare for the voyage. On the morning of Saturday, September 23rd, all the 83 Basque whalers set sail from Reykjarfjörður on 8 boats, of which some are not whaling *txalupas* but smaller ship-boats. Guðmundsson wrote that the Icelanders estimated the sea still rather rough and admired them for being able to sail in such seas. Nothing is mentioned of their journey. Probably they slept in the boat-sheds and houses on their way, small and isolated settlements on the northern Strandir, or maybe in their boats when pulled to land and had a sail over.

On 26 September, Tuesday, the sailors arrive at Leirufjörður in the Jökulfirðir. Farmer of the house Dynjandi, Gunnsteinn Gríms-son, owned a sailing vessel, *skúta,* an open and one-masted ship with a square sail. As Guðmunsson had told the whalers the vessel was nothing to sail overseas with. They slaughter a barren cow and stay there two nights. At this point, following Grímsson's suggestions, Agirre and Telleria's men separated from Villafranca's men, taking Gunnsteinn's cutter and sailing towards Sugandafjörður, and from there to Ingjaldssandur in Önundarfjörður where they spent one night. Sometime later, they reached Patreksfjörður. There they oc-cupied the Danish merchants' houses at Vatneyri and Geirseyri and they were helped by Björn Magnússon, Ari's brother, and Ragnheiður, his mother, "who throughout the winter, God bless them, took pity on these poor foreigners that were stuck so far away from home."[91]

Villafranca's men, in four boats, navigated to Ísafjörður and from there to the island of Æðey, property of Ari Magnússon. From Æðey, Villafranca and part of his crew went in two of the *txalupas* to Sandeyri where they processed a whale they had caught. The other

---

91   Guðmundsson, Jón, *Fjölmóður.* Verse 117, Available at: http://bragi.info/ ljod.php?ID=2248. Spanish version Huxley, Selma (Ed.), *Itsasoa. El mar de Euskalerria. La naturaleza, el hombre y su historia*, Etor, Donostia, 1987, p. 314.

two boats sailed to Bolungarvík on the evening of Michaelmas, September 29, and the crew of these two *txalupas* spent the night there. The next morning they followed the coast towards Staður in Súgandafjörður. "They reached Staður in the Súgandafjörður and pillaged as much as they could from the pastor. Then they swept past all the way to Þingeyri with what they had stolen and taken."[92]

The massacre

When the Dýrafjörður inhabitants saw the fourteen men of Villafranca's crew going towards Þingeyri, they gathered about thirty armed men to attack them when they returned towards the mouth of the fjord. If Agirre's, Telleria's and Villafranca's ships had not perished in the storm, nothing would have happened. The mariners would have left Iceland and no one would have known anything about the illegal permits that Magnússon had sold to the whalers. But after the shipwrecks, 83 desperate men had started their pilgrimage carrying with them the letters written by Rev. Grímsson and the illegal permits issued by the magistrate.[93]

It had happened only one year earlier. The magistrate of the Snæfellsnes peninsula, Gísli Þórðarson, had given a permission to catch falcons to an English trader. Unfortunately he also made trade on Snæfellsnes when catching his falcons and the Danish merchants arrested him and confiscated his goods. The Englishman send a letter of grief to his king who wrote again to his cousin, Christian the IV of Denmark. Gísli was dismissed from his position and a penalty fee was doomed on him at the Alþingi in 1614. He had had no authority to give the license for falcon-catching in the first place – and then he had bad luck, without the royal involvement he would have probably not punished so severely. It is very likely that

---

92   Irujo, Xabier; Matthíasdóttir, Hólmfríður (Eds.), *1615: Baskavígin / Euskal baleazaleen sarraskia / La masacre de los balleneros vascos / The Massacre of Basque Whalers*, Euskal Erria, Montevideo, 2015, p. 275.
93   Ibid., p. 236.

Ari felt his position threatened, if his dealing with the Basques was uncovered and known to the Alþingi.[94]

So the men hunt started. At this time in Iceland it was legal to carry out murders unpunished.[95] As Guðmunsson refers Ari must have known about the shipwreck and the intentions of the Basque whalers and had a few days to make the necessary arrangements. A man can ride a horse from Ögur to Dýrafjörður over the heights in one day. The richest house there was the house of Núpur and the farmer of Núpur was Jón Gissurarson, second cousin to Ari. Most probably Ari sent a word to his cousin and organized the massacre. Ari gathered some men, among them a few men capable of killing in cold blood. The uninhabited lands of the north west of Iceland had been resettled with delinquents whose crimes had been pardoned by Magnússon in order to have them live in this desolate region, and these were the ones that "had no respect for anything or anyone" and had started to steal from the whalers.[96] Tension mounted and "the servants of lies had taken the place of honoured men in the administration of justice."[97]

The two boats arrived in Dýrafjörður and the Basque whalers broke in the trading post house at Þingeyri. The merchant has already sailed home, but there was some dried fish and salt in the hut. After that they sail or row to Fjallaskagi, which is on the northern side of Dýrafjörður, facing the open sea. Here the sailors found a boat lending and a fishermen's hut at the head of the fjord, at Fjallaskagi. Five of them sat vigil for the boats while the others slept.

Bjarni Jónsson told Rev. Grímsson what happened next, the night of the first massacre, who later told Guðmundsson. The peasants of Dýrafjörður gather a troop, they come at night, surround the hut, kill the night watchmen and also everybody in the hut. A minimum

94 Koivukari, Tapio, "The Slaying of Spaniards: Current of Events and Reflections", unpublished manuscript.
95 Guðmundsson, Jón, *Fjölmóður.* http://bragi.info/ljod.php?ID=2248. Spanish version in Huxley, Selma (Ed.), *Itsasoa. El mar de Euskalerria. La naturaleza, el hombre y su historia*, Etor, Donostia, 1987, p. 314.
96 Stanza No. 64 of *Fjölmóður.* In, Sigursveinsson, Sigurður, "La trágica muerte de Martin de Villafranca en Islandia", in Huxley, Selma (Ed.), *Itsasoa. El mar de Euskalerria. La naturaleza, el hombre y su historia*, Etor, Donostia, 1987, p. 304.
97 Ibid.

of thirteen men were killed that night. The corpses were cut, "desecrated and sunk to the ocean, as they were the worst of heathens but not innocent and poor Christians", wrote Guðmundsson.

One boy named Garcia (Garcius) is said to have survived the massacre; he had hidden himself somewhere. Then he was seen from the vessel sailing southward and was rescued by the men of captains Agirre and Telleria who sailed to Patreksfjörður and stayed there over the winter. And they must have told the story to Icelanders there, because the survival of the boy is mentioned both by Jón Guðmundsson and by Ólafur Jónsson, Pastor at Sandar, in the *Spænsku vísur*.[98]

In the meantime, the other two *txalupas* from Villafranca's ship had reached Æðey, an island property of Ari Magnússon,[99] whose main farm, Ögur, faces Æðey from across the fjord. Pedro 'the prudent', the pilot, was among this group. They unloaded their boats in Æðey and settled down there. Not knowing what had happened to the other mariners, they set out to fish and hunt whales.

On October 8, a Sunday by Julian reckoning (Thursday in the Gregorian calendar), Magnússon summoned a tribunal of twelve jury members in Súðavík bý Álftafjörður by Djúpið.[100] There are 12 court members and Ari and with a reference to the King's letter since the spring of the same year, they condemn the shipwreck survivors and turn them into outlaws. In the judgement of Súðavík can be read that the judgment is done mostly in a preventive sense, thinking that if they are allowed to be here, they will start plundering forcing thus the local people to flee to the mountains in the wintertime. In sum, the decision was not taken based on actual deeds, but rather

98   Sigursveinsson, Sigurður, "La trágica muerte de Martin de Villafranca en Islandia", in Huxley, Selma (Ed.), *Itsasoa. El mar de Euskalerria. La naturaleza, el hombre y su historia*, Etor, Donostia, 1987, p. 289.

99   Ari Magnússon bought the island of Æðey on April 7, 1608. See Róbertsson, Gísli Baldur, „Nýtt af Bjarna Jónssyni lögbókarskrifara á Snæfjallaströnd", Gripla, 21, 2010, p. 350.

100   Jónsson, Már, "The Killings of 1615: Antecedents and Plausible Causes". In Irujo, Xabier; Miglio, Viola (Eds.), *Basque Whaling in Iceland in the 17th Century: Legal Organization, Cultural Exchange and Conflicts*, Barandiaran Chair of Basque Studies/University of California, Santa Barbara and Strandagaldur, 2015, p. 145. See also Ólason, Páll Eggert, „Menn og menntir siðaskiptaaldarinnar á Íslandi", III, Bókaverslun Ársæls Árnasonar, Reykjavík, 1924, pp. 501-502.

in future threats. "He gathered together people from Sandeyri, his region, to murder and kill" and forced people to face the mariners willingly or pay a fine. Some people went willingly because they had been promised 'spoils of war', but others were not so eager to join in.

And thus were the Basques condemned to be killed whenever met. And Ari sent out the command of mobilization, rose an army of more than fifty men from Djúpið and five men come from Strandir, followed by their pastor Jón Grímsson. More than fifty armed men gathered at Ari Magnússon's farm on October 10, the last Tuesday of summer[101]. Guðmundsson provides the names of some of the people that participated in the massacre: Ari Magnússon and his son Magnús Arason, Björn Sveinsson, a young farmhand from Ari's household, Bjarni Jónsson and the pastors Jón Grímsson and Jón Þorleifsson from Snæfjöll. In *Fjölmóður* he also mentions a certain Grímur.

Ready to depart, weather turned suddenly bad and men are forced to sit in Ögur, probably in the fishing huts of Ögurnes, and wait. According to Meteorologist Einar Sveinbjörnsson, the wind was likely of northeast, which can stay many days and be rather harsh in the Djúpið at this time of the year. When the wind finally settles, in the afternoon of October 13th, Friday, Magnússon sent a scout boat of three men over to Æðey. The patrol returned and informed the Governor that captain Villafranca and twelve of his men, unaware of what happening,[102] were occupied in processing

---

101 Icelandic seasons are traditionally just two: winter (from about October 20 to April 20), and summer.

102 Ólafur Jónsson, Pastor at Sandar, wrote in the *Spænsku vísur* that, probably knowing what had happened to their men at Dýrafjörður, Martin de Villafranca and his crew came from Æðey to Ögur when Ari was still in Súðavík on October 8th or 9th. Armed with knives they told Ari's wife that they would kill Ari if he did not leave them alone, and that they pretended crying. Then they went back to Æðey. This incident was not referred by Jón Guðmundsson and raises many doubts. If true, we must ask, why should captain Villafranca do such a thing? Someone had told them by gestures and mimes what had happened by risking his or her own life? What was their intention, what would they have done if Ari had been at home? Negotiate with him? Kill him and take revenge? Take him hostage? According to Jónsson's account Ari's wife Kristín was at home and they could have easily taken her hostage. But they did not. Taking into account the lack of credibility of Jonsson's *Spænsku vísur*, most probably this never happened.

a whale that had hunted in order to have some food for facing the winter at Sandeyri, on the shore, about 10 kilometers westward of Æðey. Villafranca's men must have used the calming wind when they spotted the whale. If the wind was North-east, the Snæfjall north of Djúpið offered a shelter from the wind.

At twilight Magnússon's men rowed from Ögur to Æðey. They hear from the inhabitants of the island that Peter the Pilot had kept a man in outlook but that had called him inside. Two men were sleeping in the hut, Peter and Lazaro, who was said to be a very thick man, probably the cook of the ship. A woman was sent in with a lamp to see how many men were in and then a number of men stepped in and killed both Peter and Lazaro. Another three men in the blacksmith's shop were also slaughtered. Guðmundsson wrote that they were the barber, the washer-boy and the "reykjaþrællinn" or literally the "smoke-slave", probably the person in charge of the melting pots. The men at Æðey were thus the ones who did not take part in the actual hunting of the whale. Guðmundsson refers to 'four mariners' and a cabin boy on Æðey in *A True Account*, but in *Fjölmóður* he wrote that there were three men in the house and three in the smithy, therefore five to six people were killed at Æðey.

> [127] A cudgel smashed Lazarus's head
> and then Pedro's brow.
> [128] An cut made by a sharp and thick pollaxe
> crossed his face under the eyes;
> Then quickly again close to his heart,
> he was passed through with the spike.
> He fell asleep into death's embrace
> that night.
> [129] The youngster's head was cleft asunder
> and his legs cut off at the knees;
> Those three companions
> defended themselves bravely,
> but died all the same that night.[103]

---

103 Guðmundsson, Jón, *Fjölmóður.* In Huxley, Selma (Ed.), *Itsasoa. El mar de Euskalerria. La naturaleza, el hombre y su historia*, Etor, Donostia, 1987, p. 314.

"The one that told the story saw all of this from the door of the house" wrote Guðmundsson. After their death, the corpses were stripped naked, brought to the cliffs, bound in bunches of two and three and thrown to the sea from a cliff on the west side of Æðey. After the killing, the men took their time to search for valuable belongings. They found a small bundle on a string around the neck of Peter the Pilot. It was supposed to be his "magic". They also found some chips of red wood in there, probably a relic or personal memories.

The wind was rising again, now from south-east, which can be very hard and take only few hours. That very night between Friday October 13 and Saturday October 14, the punitive expedition rowed from Ísafjörður to Sandeyri.

The wind was so hard that they could not dare out to the sea, no more than they just made it from Æðey over to the Snæfjallaströnd, over the sound. There is a pasture hut for the sheep of Æðey and a landing site for a boat or boats. Men started marching westward to Sandeyri, in darkness, and a lightning stroke over. Ari said that it was a sign of victory from God, but this view was not shared by everyone. At least someone said to Guðmundsson that this was a sign of the wrath of God, a sign that they were doing the works of evil. The way to Sandeyri is 10 kilomters. It was raining, and the wind was blowing.

Magnússon's band surrounded the buildings on Sandeyri. Jón from Snæfjöll, Jón Grímsson, and a third pastor stood around him with some armed men. They got to know that Martin was staying with two other men in a shed, burned a small fire, while others were in the farmhouse. Ari's men shot at the window and the door of the shed. After a while captain Villafranca said in Latin that they did not deserve such a treatment, that they had done nothing wrong. Pastor Jón Grímsson answered that Martin had threatened to hang him. Villafranca asked for pardon and Grímsson agreed and asked mercy for them. Following the negotiation, Villafranca laid out his Carabine, stepped out and kneed in front of Magnússon and the priests. However, while he was down in his kneels and capitulating, someone hit him with an axe, breaking him the collar bone. Martin jumped up and ran to the shore, and some men went after him. He ran into the sea, started swimming, turned on his back and sang in Latin. Everybody admired how fast he run, that he could swim (most Icelanders did not) and that his song was so beautiful that nobody had heard anything like it before.

Some men took the boats and tried to catch him by rowing. However, "he was swimming like a seal or a trout", diving under the boat when it started to reach him. "They pursued him with great zeal on board the ships, but he swam like a seal or a fish. Then one of the men boasted of hitting him with a stone on the head while he swam under the boat once, and they all agreed that Björn Sveinsson, Ari's farmhand had eventually hit him on the forehead, and that only then he had lost some strength and some of his capacity to swim, and not before. But it is uncertain, as it was also said, that he had reached for the boat and then his hand had been hewn off. After the stone's blow to the head, most of his strength had gone. He was then dragged ashore, and stripped naked. Our pastor was closest to him and he said that what stood out most in his memory was his bravery, and his soldier-like demeanor because when his naked body lay stark naked facing upwards, and he was still moaning, one of the men stabbed him in the chest and slashed him down to his genitals, Martín sprang up one more time, turned face-down and then died, his bowels having fallen out of his body. The armed men all ran up to him and wanted to see the man and his blood. His body was then taken out to sea and sunk deep in the fjord, but the day after he had resurfaced at Ögurshólm, where he was then buried under a cairn."[104]

By the same time the wind fell down. This was noticed and men said, that Martin must have possessed some magic energy. Guðmundsson's description is very touching and we can assume that he was a man of very special charisma. The story of his death has traits of a cosmic tragedy.

---

104 Irujo, Xabier; Matthíasdóttir, Hólmfríður (Eds.), *1615: Baskavígin / Euskal baleazaleen sarraskia / La masacre de los balleneros vascos / The Massacre of Basque Whalers*, Euskal Erria, Montevideo, 2015, pp. 281-282.

The two other men of the hut were slayed as well, among them was the man who had put the hangman's rope on Pastor Grímsson's neck. He also asked for forgiving, got it and was then killed.

Basques inside the house put stones from the open stove on the door. Icelanders made a hole in the torf roof of the house and Magnússon's seventeen-year-old son Magnús climbed on the roof. He shot the men inside one by one through the hole, a loaded Carabine was always passed on to him. Last, when everyone was shot, men entered the house and found a slightly wounded man hiding under a cow, as it was common to keep cows under the same roof in Icelandic farmhouses because of the heat.

Someone recognized the man that Icelanders called "Marteinn meinlausi" or "Martin the harmless." He was the carpenter of the ship. He kneeled in front of Magnússon who stood with three pastors (Jón Grímsson, the pastor of Ögur and the pastor of Snæfjallaströnd from Unandsdalur) and asked for mercy. Magnússon said that the man should be pardoned and that to have a carpenter at the household in Ögur would be handy. But he has hit with an axe while another person hit him from behind. Cut into two, Martin's scull fell down in two pieces.

It seems that during the march and the siege the night had also passed. Events like Martin de Villafranca's killing, and the rest of the killings, must have happened at twilight or early morning.

Despite Magnússon had promised his men a booty, he announced that the possessions of the Basque whalers belonged to the crown and that, as a consequence, as his delegate in the land, he would take care of them. The men who had participated in the massacre were left the clothes of the fallen. And added that they could do whatever they wanted with the corpses. They were desecrated: naked, their eyes were stabbed and, ears, noses and genitals cut off their bodies. Then they cut their throats open, and perforated the bodies between the hip and ribs. They bound the corpses together with ropes, back to back, so that the mutilated face and body was to be seen. Finally, the "body-bunches" were pulled to the boats and dropped into the sea.

After this Magnússon's party headed to Æðey and drunk the wine and brandy taken from the Basques. They slept there overnight, went to Ögur, drank a bit more from the governor's storages and finally went back home.

More than thirteen men died at Sandeyri but the total death toll is still uncertain, and the names of most of the victims are unknown to us. We know from the information provided by Guðmundsson that on sharing the blubber among the three ships the proportion of the crew of Villafranca against the ships of Agirre and telleria was three to four. Every seven barrels of whale oil the vessel Villafranca owed three, which represents approximately 43% of the total product. Given that Guðmundsson states that such distribution was made according to the crew of the three ships, Villafranca's ship should have a crew of around forty men out of a total of 86 sailors to the three ships. We also know that four of the eight *txalupas* in which they headed north transported Villafranca's crew. This allows us to estimate that Villafranca's crew must have been between forty and fifty men, all of whom died, except one boy.

We know that at least thirteen people died during the first massacre at Dýrafjörður; Guðmundsson refers that five or six sailors were killed at Æðey and, for his description of the massacre at Sandeyri, we know that more than thirteen people were killed there. That leaves a total death toll of between a minimum of thirty-two and an approximate maximum of about forty sailors killed in 1615.

Patreksfjörður

Agirre's and Telleria's men arrived to Vatneyri, Patreksfjörður, in the exact same place where the village of Patreksfjörður is currently located. There was a trading post and a hut there, now empty. They broke in and made a stay for the winter. They went to the bigger farmhouses and asked for charity. Most likely they got it as well as some line and hooks and were able to fish, which means that they might have some fishing equipment with them. But most probably they survived thanks to the help provided by the locals. Astonishing as it may appear, their main benefactors in Patreksfjörður were a wealthy widow, Ragnheiður Eggertsdóttir and Björn Magnússon, Ari's brother, "who throughout the winter, God bless them, took pity on these poor foreigners that were stuck so far away from home."[105] Most probably Ragnheiður and Björn were unaware of her son's deeds.

Thank to their help the Basque sailors did survive the winter in Patreksfjörður. Probably they fished and got also some supplies from the farmhouses. As for the reading of the *Spænsku vísur*, or 'Spanish Stanzas', composed by Ólafur Jónsson they did also raids north to Arnarfjörður area, and stole or ploundred supplies in Rafnseyri by Arnarfjörður. The author added that Ragnheiður had to give the sailors supplies worth thirty cows. This may be well considered an exaggeration, since a decent farm was worth no more than twenty cows.

Magnússon called up another mobilization in January, in the midst of the Icelandic winter. He marched with his troops of almost one hundred men to Dýrafjörður where they had a court meeting in the house of Mýrar on 26 January 1616. Magnússon declared through another verdict (Mýrardómur) that the other Basque whalers holed up in Patreksfjörður should also be killed, and organized another punitive expedition to execute Agirre's and Telleria's men. Thus, the Basque whalers were condemned for the second time to death. They carried on their way to Patreksfjörður, tried an ambush for plundering the Basques in Tálknafjörður and shot one escaping whaler. Then the band tried to march over to Patreksfjörður, but had to turn back on the last height between Tálknafjörður and Patreksfjörður because of a sudden blizzard. This was, of course, said to be the result of a weather sorcery made by the Basques.

In the spring the Basques hijacked an English fishing vessel and made it to set sails for Donostia. Whether they made their way home or not is not known.

---

105 Guðmundsson, Jón, *Fjölmóður.* Verse 117, Available at: http://bragi.info/ljod.php?ID=2248. Spanish version Huxley, Selma (Ed.), *Itsasoa. El mar de Euskalerria. La naturaleza, el hombre y su historia*, Etor, Donostia, 1987, p. 314.

In the summer of 1616 Magnússon held a meeting in Holt, at Önundarfjörður, where his acts were considered "right and justified". Ari Magnússon obtained this way the legal justification for the punitive expedition from the Icelandic parliament and the Supreme Court at Þingvellir in 1616. Within this historico-political context, it is likely that he himself might have requested the composition of the propaganda poems from his local versifying friends. In these poems, then, the Basque mariners would be described as criminals, bloodthirsty prowlers, aggressive troblemakers and even rapists. The local population in the Westfjords, and possibly Ari Magnússon himself, feared future retaliations from the Basques, and consequently requested two Danish warships to patrol the Icelandic shores. While the ships did arrive in 1616, no retaliation ever took place.[106]

By same time the boat *Nuestra Señora del Rosario*, a whaler ship from Donostia, was caught whaling in northern Norway by a Danish warship. The captain showed a license written and signed by a certain "Ariasman", i.e. Ari Magnússon, but the document had no legal power in Norwegian waters. Thus, Magnússon almost got into trouble, but he escaped justice again. *Nuestra Señora del Rosario* was confiscated and lied over for the winter in Copenhagen, being released only after a great deal of diplomatic paperwork.

The excavations in Hveravík by Steingrimsfjörður show that the whaling station there was used for many decades. So, the Basque did return whaling to the place. After a ten year long absence, the whalers returned to the Westfjords in 1626, when the Icelandic annals record the presence of a "French" ship, probably from Lapurdi. Magnús Rafnsson and Ragnar Edvardsson point out that records about the presence of Basque and Dutch whalers in the second part of the XVII century are common: for instance in 1656, 1662, 1663, 1673, 1677, 1678, 1683, 1685, 1689, 1690, 1691, 1695, 1698, 1699 and 1701.[107]

---

106 Irujo, Xabier; Matthíasdóttir, Hólmfríður (Eds.), *1615: Baskavígin / Euskal baleazaleen sarraskia / La masacre de los balleneros vascos / The Massacre of Basque Whalers*, Euskal Erria, Montevideo, 2015, p. 253.

107 Rafnsson, Magnús; Edvarsson, Ragnar, "Basque Whaling Around Iceland. Archeological Investigation in Strákatangi (Steingrímsfjörður)", Nátturustofa Vestfjarða & Strandagaldur, Bolungarvík/Hólmavík, 2006. Available at: http://www.galdrasyning.is/baskarnir.pdf

The 17th century was an important period of interaction between Basques and Icelanders, therefore, as expressed by Prof. Miglio, it is not surprising that the Basque-Icelandic glossaries were produced in this century and that all the four glossaries that we have found to the day were produced in the Westfjords. Both Icelanders and Basques were aware of the importance of speaking both languages for facilitating communication among them.[108] Also, the glossaries written by Basques and Icelanders as a way to understand each other and learn each other's language show that there were more and more peaceful contacts between the Basque and Icelandic people all during the 17th century. The word lists are bilingual, Icelandic on the one side and Basque on the other while some of the sentences are partly taken from English: *Me presenta for ju.... ju presenta for mi...*[109]

The last recorded whaling ship sailed to Iceland in 1712, no other Basque ship is found in the historical sources after that year: on the one hand, the loss of whale hunting and fishing rights may have been a direct cause of the Treaty of Utrecht between 1712 and 1715.

There is also a last and mysterious document in the National Archives at Copenhagen. A Danish nobleman and a diplomate "purchased" some Icelandic people from the "Bischayen" in the 1640's. The document provides seven names, most of them women. Nothing more is said of these people and we do not know why were in Basque Country, nor what happened to them next. It is anyway most likely that they got to Euskal Herria with the whalers. Some of the names are Christian names with a Basque spelling like "Hurida", which may well be "Þuríður", or "Hura", "Þóra", both female names. Most probably the yearly contacts between Basques and Icelanders generated some mixt marriages and common interests.

---

108 Knörr, Henrike, "Basque fishermen in Iceland: Bilingual vocabularies in the 17th and 18th centuries". Paper presented at the conference *Slaying of Spaniards in the West Fjords in 1615*, Dalbær Snæfjallaströnd, Iceland, June 24-25, 2006. Online at: http://www.euskaltzaindia.net/dok/euskera/66537.pdf

109 Miglio, Viola G., "'Go shag a horse!': The 17th–18th Century Basque-Icelandic Glossaries Revisited," Journal of the North Atlantic, Volume 1, Issue 1, Eagle Hill Institute, 2008, pp. 25-36. Available at http://www.bioone.org/doi/abs/10.3721/071010

Bibliography

Barkham, Michael M., "La industria pesquera en el País Vasco peninsular al principio de la Edad Moderna: ¿Una edad de oro", *Itsas Memoria. Revista de Estudios Marítimos del País Vasco*, 3, pp. 29–75, 2000.

Dennis, Andrew; Foote, Peter; Perkins, Richard (Eds.), *Laws of Early Iceland: Grágás I*, Univ. of Manitoba Press, 2014.

Gassmann, Günther; Oldenburg, Mark W., *Historical Dictionary of Lutheranism*, The Scarecrow Press, Toronto, 2011.

Horrebow, Niels, *The Natural History of Iceland: Containing a Particular and Accurate Account of the Different Soils, Burning Mountains, Minerals, Vegetables, Metals, Stones, Beasts, Birds, and Fishes; Together with the Disposition, Customs, and Manner of Living of the Inhabitants*, A. Linde, 1758.

Huxley, Selma (Ed.), *Itsasoa. El mar de Euskalerria. La naturaleza, el hombre y su historia*, Etor, Donostia, 1987.

Irujo, Xabier and Hólmfríður Matthíasdóttir (Eds.), *1615: Spánverjavígin / Euskal baleazaleen hilketa / La matanza de los vascos / The slaying of the Basques*, Forlagið, Reykjavík, 2015.

Irujo, Xabier and Hólmfríður Matthíasdóttir (Eds.), *1615: Spánverjavígin / Euskal baleazaleen hilketa / La matanza de los vascos / The slaying of the Basques*, Forlagið, Reykjavík, 2015.

Irujo, Xabier and Viola Miglio (Eds.), *Basque Whaling in Iceland in the 17th Century: Legal Organization, Cultural Exchange and Conflicts*, University of California, Santa Barbara/Barandiaran Chair of Basque Studies and Strandagaldur, 2015.

Jóhannesson, Guðni Th., *The History of Iceland*, Greenwood, Santa Barbara (Cal) 2013.

Jónsson, Már. 2015. "Introducción", en, Irujo, Xabier; Matthíasdóttir, Hólmfríður (Eds.), *1615: Spánverjavígin / Euskal baleazaleen hilketa* / *La matanza de los vascos* / *The slaying of the Basques*, Forlagið, Reykjavík, 2015, pp. 157-180.

Karlsson, Gunnar, *The History of Iceland*, University of Minnesota Press, Minneapolis, 2000.

Knörr, Henrike, "Basque fishermen in Iceland: Bilingual vocabularies in the 17th and 18th centuries". Paper presented at the conference *Slaying of Spaniards in the West Fjords in 1615*, Dalbær Snæfjallaströnd, Iceland, June 24-25, 2006. Online at: http://www.euskaltzaindia.net/dok/euskera/66537.pdf

Koivukari, Tapio, "The Slaying of Spaniards: Current of Events and Reflections", unpublished manuscript.

Kristjánsson, Jónas, *Spánverjavígin 1615. Sönn frásaga eftir Jón Guðmundsson lærða og Víkinga rímur*, Möller, Copenhagen, 1950.

Miglio, Viola G., "'Go shag a horse!': The 17th–18th Century Basque-Icelandic Glossaries Revisited," Journal of the North Atlantic, Volume 1, Issue 1, Eagle Hill Institute, 2008, pp. 25-36. Available at http://www.bioone.org/doi/abs/10.3721/071010

Pencak, William, *The Conflict of Law and Justice in the Icelandic Sagas*, Rodopi, Amsterdam, 1995.

Rafnsson, Magnús and Ragnar Edvarsson, "Basque Whaling Around Iceland. Archeological Investigation in Strákatangi (Steingrímsfjörður)", Nátturustofa Vestfjarða & Strandagaldur, Bolungarvík/Hólmavík, 2006. Available at: http://www.galdrasyning.is/baskarnir.pdf

CHAPTER FOUR

Atrocious Icelanders versus Basques. Unexpected violence or not?

Helgi Þorláksson
University of Iceland

Icelanders have often wondered why their ancestors in 1615 treated Basque whalers in such a horrific way, brutally slaughtering 31 of them and maltreating their corpses. [110] It amazes modern Icelanders how militant and cruel their ancestors were.[111] People like to see their ancestors in 1615 as we believe Icelandic peasants were in later times, peace loving, hospitable towards strangers, never harming

---

110 Two groups of the Basques were killed in 1615, first 13, then 18, and at least in the latter case this was an organized military action under the leadership of the magnate and sheriff (sýslumaður) Ari Magnússon.
111 On such sentiments see Torfi Tulinius,"Voru Spánverjavígin fjöldamorð?" Ársrit Sögufélags Ísfirðinga *2006*, 103-18. To Torfi the killings in 1615 resemble a massacre; on massacres see Alan A. Tulchin, "Massacres during the French Wars of Religion", in Ritual and Violence: Natalie Zemon Davis and Early Modern France, eds. Graeme Murdock, Penny Roberts, and Andrew Spicer (Oxford: Oxford University Press, 2012), 100-126.

other people on purpose. However, the same does not apply for Iceland around 1600, peasants sometimes fought outside churches on Sundays, carried knives and would wound their enemies. This is not startling, the Icelandic society was a feuding society, from times immemorial. And, until around 1575, manslaughter was not uncommon among the upper layers of society. Killing in revenge took place in cases when those who felt that they had been seriously offended, and their honour been tarnished, wanted to wash it by killing the offender. However, in the late Middle Ages and until around 1575 only those who could afford to pay a round sum in fines to the king for the act of killing did this. The common man could not afford to kill in revenge and had to be satisfied with beating his adversary and stab him with a knife, without killing.[112]

As late as 1570 magnates with groups of physically able men would pay visits to tenants or protégés of their adversaries, to rob their homes and beat them. A hostile visit of this kind was called heimreið in Icelandic and can be seen as a rite of violence, a part of the feuding game.[113] After c. 1575 the royal authorities would neither hear of such visits nor killings in revenge any more. Notwithstanding, physical assaults with beating and the stabbing with knives continued among high and low during the 17th century.

Foreigners were not necessarily spared. English fishermen were at the coast of Iceland around 1408, for the first time, and merchant sailors followed in their wake. The English apparently became quite common in Iceland around 1420, at least in the south and west and probably somewhat later in the north. A crew of an English vessel obviously was in trouble in the north in 1431 because they fled to the residence of the bishop at Hólar, seeking shelter there. In a letter the bishop mentions violations and remedies for damage.[114] In 1952 road-builders came upon a heap of human bones 25-30 km north of the episcopal residence. During excavations in 1953 it turned

112 Helgi Þorláksson, Frá kirkjuvaldi til ríkisvalds. Saga Íslands VI, ed. Sigurður Líndal (Reykjavík: Hið íslenska bókmenntafélag, Sögufélagið, 2003), 353-60.
113 Helgi Þorláksson, "Vald og ofurvald. Um innlent vald, erlent konungsvald og líkamlegt ofbeldi á 15. öld". Leiðarminni. Greinar gefnar út í tilefni 70 ára afmælis Helga Þorlákssonar, 8. ágúst 2015 (Reykjavík. Hið íslenska bókmenntafélag, Sögufélag, 2015), 279-95.
114 Diplomatarium islandicum, Íslenzkt fornbréfasafn IV, 477-9.

out that they were bones from at least five males, between 20 and 50 years of age, who had been thrown disgracefully into a ditch. Two of the men or even three had been beheaded. The conclusion was that these were foreigners, probably intruders in the period 1000-1500. To scholars it has seemed possible that they had something to do with the dispute and friction in 1431.[115]

During the first riots of the reformation in 1539 the foreign representative of the Danish king in Iceland, as an harbinger of protestantism, with a group of men headed for the monasteries in the south to confiscate their belongings. On their way they paid a visit to the residence of the Catholic bishop in Skálholt and were all killed by his men. This slaying was justified afterwards with a passing of a sentence for those already killed.[116]

There were more instances like this, a foreign bishop of Skálholt was drowned in 1433 at the instigation of some Icelandic magnates and all his foreign servants were killed.[117] The Icelanders also killed several of the foreign representatives of the king, for instance in 1502, 1523, 1539 and 1551, usually with their retainers. After the introduction of lutheranism, finally in 1551, and because of increased royal power such killings are not heard of anymore. However they were probably cherished in memories.

Homicides or manslaughter in revenge were not uncommon in Iceland until around 1575 when they came to an end because of royal dismay. But as pointed out above, the Icelandic society was still a feuding society around 1615. What does that mean? Even though royal power had increased it was still weak, and real state power was at an incipient stage. During clashes between neighbours they themselves would usually solve their disputes, the sheriffs (*sýslumenn*, sing sýslumaður) would hardly act unless one of the parts accused

---

115 Kristján Eldjárn and Jón Steffensen, "Ræningjadysjar og Englendingabein". Árbók Hins íslenzka fornleifafélags 1959, 92-110.
116 Jón Egilsson, Biskupa-annálar Jóns Egilssonar. Safn til sögu Íslands og íslenzkra bókmenta að fornu og nýju, 68-72 (Copenhagen: Hið íslenzka bókmentafélag). Diplomatarium islandicum, Íslenzkt fornbréfasafn X, 462-7.
117 Helgi Þorláksson,"Who governed Iceland in the first half og the 15th century? King, council and the Old Covenant", Legislation and State Formation, Norway and its Neighbours in the Middle Ages, ed Steinar Imsen (Trondheim, Akademika Publishing, 2013), 263-70.

the other and apparently that was not common. As a rule there were clashes because of material interests, over grazing lands, woods, boundaries and so on, or frictions because some words uttered were found disrespectful. One of the parts felt offended, blamed the other part for transgression and for tarnishing their honour. The other part felt insulted and answered in a harsh way. If the first part did not yield a feud had started. It was brought out into the open, made publicly known by the parts, was totally unconcealed. First the clashes were on the verbal stage, the animosity might grow, the atmosphere become chilly. If the dispute was not solved by friends and neighbours the parts became physically violent, animals might be wounded or killed and some brawl would follow, commonly on Sundays at church, and often the acts of beating with a club or a stone or stabbing or cutting the other part with a knife ensued. One of the parts might despair when violence was growing, go to law, contact the sheriff and litigate, accuse the other officially. There are some documents preserved for such cases, known to us because sheriffs were asked to intervene even though that was probably not the rule.[118]

The main carachteristics and the pattern of a feud were: a) honour was at stake; b) resort to vindictive action was found necessary; c) the parts acted in turns, after reacting a part would wait for the other to react, wait for their move before acting again; d) escalation of violence was typical; e) anger turned into hatred, each part saw the other as antisocial and declared that there were no possibilities they would ever give in to such scoundrels and would never come to a settlement; f) the dispute became a major concern of the community, mediators tried to bring about a truce; some men whom both parts trusted compelled them to settle the case. They would do it on the condition that their honour would be restored which was the rule, both kept their honour intact. All grievances were equalled out, wound against a wound and so on.

---

118 Helgi Þorláksson, "Hvað er blóðhefnd?" Sagnaþing helgað Jónasi Kristjánssyni sjötugum 10. apríl 1994, I (Reykjavík: Hið íslenzka bókmenntafélag, 1994), 389-414.

Peace was reintroduced. Men who brought about a settlement and peace were called "men of good will", the same expression would be used for them in other feuding societies.

Many years ago it occurred to me that the slaughtering of the Basques could be best accounted for within the framework of feud which I am going to explain. When the Basques were in Iceland in 1613 there were some collisions between them and the Icelanders in Strandir (Strandasýsla), nothing serious as it seems. Again in 1614 there were clashes between them and the Icelanders in Strandir and the situation was getting serious. The Basques were interested in sheep and bulls and one annal says that they took them unfreely.[119] In a letter from the king of April 30th 1615 a complaint from the Icelanders is mentioned, probably sent in 1614, the Basques are said to have plundered the inhabitants and burdened them (in Danish *røveri* and *overlast*).[120] The best source is the True Account (Sönn frásaga) by Jón *the Learned,* probably written in the autumn of 1615. There he says that in 1614 the Basques disturbed the inhabitants with their overbearing behaviour and sometimes with pilfering.[121] In the much later source, Fjölmóður, Jón says some Icelandic men he calls *strákar* (on the meaning see below) in 1614 took something unfreely from the Basques and slandered them when complaining to the sheriff, Ari Magnússon. Some Icelanders prevented the Basques from buying or taking sheep and bulls by using clubs and scythes. This Jón says in Fjölmóður.[122] According to his True Account it got worse when the Basques came back in the spring

---

119 Skarðsárannáll on "glettingar" by the Basques in 1613 (i.e. vexing or taunting the inhabitants and probably vice versa) and on damage caused by foreign robbers around Iceland, in 1614. Annálar 1400-1800 I (Reykjavík: Hið íslenzka bókmentafélag 1922-1927), 200, 201. Sjávarborgarannáll on the Basques being "meinlitlir" in 1613 (i.e. not so harmful) and quite the opposite in 1614, taking bulls and sheep unfreely, intimidating the inhabitants and acquiring their belongings, Annálar 1400-1800 IV (Reykjavík: Hið íslenzka bókmenntafélag 1940-1949).

120 Edited by Már Jónsson in his, "Aðdragandi og ástæða Spánverjavíga haustið 1615". Ársrit Sögufélags Ísfirðinga 2006, 79-80.

121 Sönn frásaga eftir Jón Guðmundsson lærða og Víkingarímur, in Spánverjavígin 1615, ed. Jónas Kristjánsson. (Copenhagen: Hið íslenzka fræðafélag, 1950), 8.

122 Fjölmóður. Ævidrápa Jóns lærða Guðmundssonar, ed. Páll Eggert Ólason. Safn til sögu Íslands V. (Reykjavík: Hið íslenzka bókmentafélag, 1916), verses 48-73 (pp. 37-55), see esp. verses 63, 65, 71, 72.

of 1615 thirteen of the crew of captain Stephen who had been in Iceland in 1614 were driven on land in a boat at a place called Eyjar, in Strandir (Strandasýsla). This lead to what Jón calls *Eyjaupphlaup*, the commotion at Eyjar. He says 30 Icelanders in Eyjar assaulted the Basques and wanted to kill them, a combat was fought out and the Icelanders fled, some of them wounded.[123] Because of this riot the crews of Stephen and Peter were alert and watched out in the following summer of 1615 and never had intercourse with the people at Reykjanes, close to Eyjar. Two members of Stephen's crew, Jón calls *strákar*, and says they wanted to take revenge and stole a sheep or some stockings from their enemies.

This at least resembles a feud. There were two groups, the parts felt offended, mutual accusations ensued, the atmosphere was chilly and the situation was prone to end in physical violence, which it did. Escalation carachterized the clashes and at least the Icelanders felt the Basques behaved in an antisocial way. The Basques only melted the fat stuff of the whales as it seems and did not have much use for all their meat. The Icelanders coveted the whale meet and instead the Basques wanted payments, in sheep and bulls. This caused collisions and accusations of debts and confiscations, groups of adversaries were forming with some escalation of violence and an open combat with wounding, the commotion at Eyjar, occurred in the spring of 1615.

There was also the third captain, Martin de Villafanca, who was there in 1615 for the first time and had difficulties in getting sheep and bulls which he coveted, providing for his crew. He did not take these difficulties lightly but all the same he was very reasonable when an Icelander knocked out one of his men with a stone. Martin saved the Icelander's life, Jón says. In the end Martin lost patience, was menacing towards the reverand of the place, at Árnes in Strandir, and one of Martin's men threatened with hanging him. This indictaes that the Basques knew the language of feud which in the present article is taken for granted.

---

123 Sönn frásaga 7-8.

In the beginning the Basques had a permisson from the sheriff, Ari Magnússon, and acted as insiders. Once the collisions started Ari's permission did not count for much and in a letter from him in 1615 (rather than 1614) to the inhabitants all intercourse and dealings with the Basques were prohibited. However some inhabitants did not pay any heed to that.[124] When Ari's permisson had lost all validity the Basques should be treated like outsiders and the royal letter of April 30th 1615 stressed that point, they were to be destroyed.

For the case of the Basques two things are of interest, seen in the context of feud, on the one hand that around 1600 men were sentenced for using the word *strákur* for their adversaries. And on the other hand, addressing your adversary like he was an animal was very serious, for instance as a dog or call him a bitch or a mare. There was a tariff for how much each word would cost if you were sentenced for expressing them.[125] This is known from Norway as well, the most common derogatory words there were dog and mare or horse, like in Iceland. The meaning most probably was that the adversary, addressed in such a way, was seen as having transgressed the boundaries between culture and nature, crossed the line of acceptable behaviour.[126]

If the offended party decided not to sue to redress such defamatory expressions and instead assaulted in revenge their reaction had to be on the same scale, for instance a blow and a wound that would cost something similar to the degrading remark, usually somewhat higher; this was the pattern of a feud. To call a man *strákur* most probably meant that he was seen as antisocial, was irresponsible, even criminal.

A peasant would not be called *strákur* by his peasant neighbour unless they had been quarrelling, the atmosphere had become chilly and the peasant neighbour was convinced that the other was dishon-

---

124 Sönn frásaga, 7.
125 In manuscripts like Lbs. 69 4to and Lbs. 63 4to (The National Library, Reykjavík).
126 Erling Sandmo, Voldsamfunnets undergang. Om disiplineringen av Norge på 1600-tallet (Oslo: Universitetsforlaget, 1999), 110-11. Jørn Sandnes, Kniven, ølet og æren. Kriminalitet og samfunn i Norge på 1500- og 1600-tallet, 1. utgave, 2. opplag, (Oslo: Universitetsforlaget, 1993), 82-3.

est and cheated or broke law. And the other neighbour, addressed in such a way, was expected to react. Such were the norms in a society where the authorities were weak, most men were on their own and had to defend themselves.

In the case of the Basques the word *strákur* is used for them in the sources, the poems Víkingarímur and the Spönsku vísur. Another serious word is *skálkur* and is used for them in both poems.[127] Jón *the Learned* even though he was friendly towards the Basques, also uses the word *strákur* for some of them and furthermore for some Icelanders who he says stole from the Basques.[128] Already in 1614 the word *strákur* would generally have been found fitting and applicable for the Basques, at least soem of them. Tension was building, mistrust in all probability caused many Icelanders to see at least some of the Basques as dangerous. And when leading people in 1615 decided to take the situation seriously, officially it turned into hostility, it was *us* against *them*. In the sentence passed in Súðavík on October eighth in 1615 the verdict was that the Basques were evildoers, outsiders, in Icelandic they were called óþjóð, quite derogatory.[129] Jón *the Learned* was seen as a traitor since he had not shown solidarity with his own people; he was aware of this and fled..

This was a state of feud and accordingly many Icelanders would have seen the Basques as contemptible. In Víkingarímur the word *hundur* is used for them, meaning dog, they were killed like dogs. And after one of the Basques had been killed the poet calls his corpse *slátur* which is used of dead sheep or cattle.[130] It is obvious that the Basques were killed and treated afterwards like animals, Jón *the Learned* plainly states this. It is nothing the poet of Víkingarímur made up. In his True Account Jón says that the Basques were killed with axes, clubs and pikes, were undressed, their corpses were parted and cut into pieces, their innards or guts were let out and what was left he calls *krof*. It means the body, for instance of a sheep, when

---

127 Víkinga rímur in Spánverjavígin 1615, ed. Jónas Kristjánsson, part I, verses 13 (strákur), 14 (strákur); part III, verse 56 (skálkur), (Copenhagen. Hið íslenzka fræðafélag, 1950). Spönsku vísur in Ólafur Davíðsson, verses 27 (strákalýður), 36 (strákskapur), 55 (strákur).
128 Sönn frásaga 7, 18.
129 Alþingisbækur Íslands IV (Reykjavík: Sögufélag, 1920-1924), 311
130 Víkinga rímur, part II, verses 50 (hundur), 49 (slátur).

its entrails and offal have been removed, in one word a carcass.[131] He was not present he says but was told that the genitals of the dead Basques were chopped off, their ears sliced off and their eyes gouged out.In Fjölmóður he repeats the same without any reservations.[132] Jón feared that he might be killed in a similar way, his house broken and he himself pierced during the night.[133] And the Basques were not burried in graves like Christian, human beings, they were thrown into the sea. It turns out that one of the Iceanders had a gun but it was hardly used. The reason might be that animals were not usually shot when killed at this time.

Jón *the Learned* would have been fit for the role of "a man of good will", to bring about peace. In a bilateral society such a role was important to end a feud; feuds were even seen as a way to let steam out and prepare for peace. In the case of outsiders feuds could develop differently and Jón did not feel his mediation and pacification was desired.

There is little reason to think it was Ari Magnússon's idea to treat the Basques as animals, the Dýrfirðingar, at a distance from Ari's home area, did this on their own when some of the shipwrecked Basques turned up in their district, robbing and stealing. They slaughtered them on October 5th, Ari had a sentence passed for the Basques on the 8th. He could not have known that the Basques would turn up in Dýrafjörður and can hardly have sent any orders there. And neither can the royal letter of April 30th explain the slaughtering in Dýrafjörður even though it says the Basques were to be destroyed; in it there are no prescriptions for them being treated like animals. Also when Ari promised to be lenient towards Martin de Villafranca his men would not hear of it.

The idea seems to have been near at hand to treat the Basques like animals when they were killed and their corpses mutilated. Why were they treated like this? Jón *the Learned* mentions one reason, says their bodies were maltreated to mock them.[134] Such a treat-

---

131 Sönn frásaga, 18, 20, 23, 25 (krof)..
132 Sönn frásaga 27. Fjölmóður, verse 151.
133 Fjölmóður, verse 167.
134 Sönn frásaga 27.

ment of enemies is well known from Italy in the 16th century. In his book *Mad Blood Stirring* Edward Muir studied common frictions between groups of men in Italy. He points out that contemporaries understood such conflicts as aspects of vendettas. Muir writes, " ... [P]articipants in vendettas followed certain patterns, especially in how they performed acts of violence. Killers ... maximized the amount of blood shed, frequently by dismembering the victim or feeding him to animals".[135] The implication was that entrails of animals would often be given to dogs. Muir points out that during vendettas or feuds butchery of animals was a model for the killing of enemies. He adds that this was done in order to dehumanize the enemies as potentially dangerous outsiders.[136]

In his later book *Ritual in Early Modern Europe* Muir further discusses the same theme. There he writes for instance, "In many parts of the Mediterranean feuding constituted the principal framework for all social relationships".[137] However, during the 16th century state-power increased and the authorities took over punishments, and vendettas or feuds were on the wane with their ideas of personal revenge and personal honour to defend. On the other hand, for their official punishments authorities adopted the same feuding methods of degrading the human body through corporeal abuse and dismemberment.[138] The English official method of drawing, hanging and quartering the body is an example. This is how traitors and heretics were treated.

During the 16th century religious wars in France such a treatment of enemy corpses was common, both among Huguenots and Catholics, mutilation of bodies, disembowelment and other acts of apparent butchery.[139] Some scholars find religious reasons for such a treatment. In Iceland at least the ritual frame of feud can better explain the slaughtering of the Basques.

---

135 Edward Muir, *Mad Blood Stirring. Vendetta & Factions in Friuli during the Renaissance.* xxiv (Baltimore & London: The John Hopkins University Press, 1993).
136 Edward Muir, *Mad Blood Stirring*, xxviii-xxix, 237-8
137 Edward Muir, *Ritual in Early Modern Europe*. Second Edition (Cambridge, New York: Cambridge University Press, 2005), 106.
138 Edward Muir, *Ritual in Early Modern Europe*, 111.
139 Penny Roberts, "Peace, Rituals, and Sexual Violence during the Religious Wars", *Ritual and Violence*, 80, 82-3.

Even though usually just a few men were killed at a time during vendettas in Italy, once in a while the number could increase. Also in Iceland groups that were defined as dangerous and hostile outsiders could be killed. In 1539 not only the royal representative was killed, the foreigner mentioned before, but also at least eight of his retainers; the leader was found to have offended the bishop in Skálholt with some abusive words. This was found very grave and a reason enough to have the leader killed.[140] Stains on the honour of the bishop had to be washed off with the blood of the representative, feuding became the framework of the events. He was slain together with his retinue of servants and bodyguards who were aso found guilty as thieves. However, usually in feuds the leader and his men were seen as one. These men did not get Christian burials, their bodies were placed in cairns, like they were pagans or social outcasts.[141]

In 1551 another foreign representative of the king, a Dane, was killed in revenge together with at least 13 of his retainers, most of them Danes and one being his young son. The main source maintains that they did not get a Christian burial and two of the deceased are said to have been beheaded since they were reported to have turned into ghosts or spectres.[142] Vindictive actions were found necessary and the deceased were defined as outsiders, all based on the principles of feuding. This reminds one of the foreigners who were excavated in 1953 in the north and had been beheaded, possibly Englishmen. They did not get Christian burials. The same goes for the two groups of the Basques in 1615, one of 13, the other of 18.

In 1579 some foreign pirates turned up in West Iceland. This made the sheriff Magnús Jónsson very concerned and he urged his countrymen to prepare for fighting foreigners.[143] He was the father of Ari Magnússon the magnate who was in charge of the slaughtering of the Basques in 1615.

---

140 *Diplomatarium islandicum, Íslenzkt fornbréfasafn* X, 464.
141 Jón Egilsson, Biskupa-annálar Jóns Egilssonar, 70, 71.
142 Jón Egilsson, Biskupa-annálar Jóns Egilssonar, 99
143 Vopnadómur in *Alþingisbækur Íslands* I (Reykjavík: Sögufélag, 1912-1914), 438-44.

Such groups of men, seen as hostile outsiders, did not necessarily have to be foreign, could very well be domestic groups of thieves and other malefactors, for instance in 1545.[144] And bodies of convicts could be dismembered or quartered as happend to a famous muderer in 1596. His body parts were spiked, stuck on sticks or poles for display. Something similar occurred in 1635.[145] However, these examples of punishments for thieves and muderers have nothing to do with feud, thieves and murderers were secretive, did not want their actions to be known as was the rule with feuding men. Source informants had no reason to see their acts from the point of view of feuds. In the case of foreigners who were seen as outsiders the framework of feuds was found applicable. And so did for instance those who passed the verdict for the royal representative in 1539. I suppose that those who took revenge for Bishop Jón Arason in 1551 saw themselves as feuding and therefore treated the Danish representative and his men in the way they did.

To treat the Basques like animals was intended to convey meaning, they were seen as guilty, trespassers of the boundaries between culture and nature. The expressions used for them, like *strákur*, suggest that they were seen as guilty outsiders. Accordingly they were dishonoured, stripped of their clothing and quartered and denied Christian burials. Thus they were treated like animals. For those who know medieval feud and its 16th century context the violence in 1615 is not so startling.

One hundred years later state power had increased, Iceland was much changed and foreigners had little reason to fear any massacre.

---

144 Páll Sigurðsson *Svipmyndir úr réttarsögu* (Reykjavík: Bókaútgáfan Skjaldborg, 1992), 202-4
145 Páll Sigurðsson, *Svipmyndir úr réttarsögu,* 157; see also 144, 262.

Bibliography

Alþingisbækur Íslands I, 1570-1581. Reykjavík: Sögufélag, 1912-1914.

Alþingisbækur Íslands IV, 1606-1619. Reykjavík: Sögufélag, 1920-1924.

Annálar 1400-1800 I. Reykjavík: Hið íslenzka bókmentafélag, 1922-1927.

Annálar 1400-1800 IV. Reykjavík: Hið íslenzka bókmenntafélag 1940-1949.

Diplomatarium islandicum, Íslenzkt fornbréfasafn IV, 1265-1449. Copenhagen: Hið íslenzka bókmentafélag, 1897.

Diplomatarium islandicum, Íslenzkt fornbréfasafn X, 1169-1542, Reykjavík: Hið íslenzka bókmentafélag, 1911-1921.

Fjölmóður. Ævidrápa Jóns lærða Guðmundssonar með inngangi og athugasemdum, edited by Páll Eggert Ólason. *Safn til sögu Íslands og íslenzkra bókmenta* V, Reykjavík: Hið íslenzka bókmentafélag, 1916.

Helgi Þorláksson, "Hvað er blóðhefnd?" *Sagnaþing helgað Jónasi Kristjánssyni sjötugum 10. apríl 1994*, I, 389-414. Reykjavík: Hið íslenzka bókmenntafélag, 1994.

Helgi Þorláksson, Frá kirkjuvaldi til ríkisvalds. *Saga Íslands* VI, edited by Sigurður Líndal, 353-60. Reykjavík: Hið íslenska bókmenntafélag, Sögufélagið, 2003.

Helgi Þorláksson,"Who governed Iceland in the first half of the 15th century? King, council and the Old Covenant", *Legislation and State Formation, Norway and its Neighbours in the Middle Ages*, eited by Steinar Imsen, Norgesveldet. Occasional Papers No. 4. Rostra Books – Trondheim Studies in History, edited by Per Hærnes, 263-86. Trondheim: Akademika Publishing, 2013.

Helgi Þorláksson, "Vald og ofurvald. Um innlent vald, erlent konungsvald og líkamlegt ofbeldi á 15. öld". *Leiðarminni. Greinar gefnar út í tilefni 70 ára afmælis Helga Þorlákssonar, 8. ágúst 2015*, 279-95. Reykjavík: Hið íslenska bókmenntafélag, Sögufélag, 2015.

Jón Egilsson, Biskupa-annálar Jóns Egilssonar. *Safn til sögu Íslands og íslenzkra bókmenta að fornu og nýju*, 68-72. Copenhagen: Hið íslenzka bókmentafélag.

Kristján Eldjárn and Jón Steffensen, "Ræningjadysjar og Englendinga-bein". Árbók Hins íslenzka fornleifafélags 1959, 92-110.

Már Jónsson, "Aðdragandi og ástæða Spánverjavíga haustið 1615". Ársrit Sögufélags Ísfirðinga 2006, 57-95.

Muir, Edward, *Mad Blood Stirring. Vendetta & Factions in Friuli during the Renaissance.* Baltimore and London: The John Hopkins University Press, 1993.

Muir, Edward, *Ritual in Early Modern Europe.* Second Edition. Cambridge, New York: Cambridge University Press, 2005.

Ólafur Davíðsson, "Víg Spánverja á Vestfjörðum 1615 og „Spönsku vísur" eptir séra Ólaf á Söndum". *Tímarit Hins íslenzka bókmenntafjelags* 16 (1895), 88-163.

Páll Sigurðsson *Svipmyndir úr réttarsögu. Þættir um land og sögu í ljósi laga og réttarframkvæmdar.* Reykjavík: Bókaútgáfan Skjaldborg, 1992.

Roberts, Penny, "Peace, Rituals, and Sexual Violence during the Religious Wars", *Ritual and Violence: Natalie Zemon Davis and Early Modern France,* edited by Graeme Murdock, Penny Roberts, and Andrew Spicer, 75-99. *Past and Present* Supplements. Supplement 7, 2012. Oxford: Oxford University Press, 2012.

Sandnes, Jørn, *Kniven, ølet og æren. Kriminalitet og samfunn i Norge på 1500- og 1600-tallet*, 1. utgave, 2. opplag. Oslo: Universitetsforlaget, 1993.

Sandmo, Erling, *Voldssamfunnets undergang. Om disiplineringen av Norge på 1600-tallet* Det blå bibliotek. Oslo: Universitetsforlaget, 1999.

Spönsku vísur, see Ólafur Davíðsson.

Sönn frásaga eftir Jón Guðmundsson lærða og Víkinga rímur, in *Spánverjavígin 1615*, edited by Jónas Kristjánsson. Íslenzk rit síðari alda, 4. Copenhagen: Hið íslenzka fræðafélag, 1950.

Torfi Tulinius, "Voru Spánverjavígin fjöldamorð?" Ársrit Sögufélags Ísfirðinga 2006, 103-18.

Tulchin, Alan A., "Massacres during the French Wars of Religion". In *Ritual and Violence: Natalie Zemon Davis and Early Modern France*, edited by Graeme Murdock, Penny Roberts, and Andrew Spicer, 100-125. *Past and Present* Supplements. Supplement 7, 2012. Oxford: Oxford University Press, 2012.

Víkinga rímur, Sönn frásaga eftir Jón Guðmundsson lærða og Víkinga rímur, in *Spánverjavígin 1615*, edited by Jónas Kristjánsson. Íslenzk rit síðari alda, 4. Copenhagen: Hið íslenzka fræðafé-lag, 1950.

CHAPTER FIVE

In the Footsteps of Jón the Learned

Paper delivered at an international
conference at the National and University
Library of Iceland on April 20-22, 2015.

Hjörleifur Guttormsson

Abstract

This paper traces the travels of Jón *lærði* (1574–1658) from the
Strandir region in northwestern Iceland, down the west coast and
to Fljótsdalshérað, in the east of the country, with the aid of maps
and photographs. Some of the moves described are speculative because exact records are not always available. A comparison is made
between the natural landscapes in the east and the northwest, where
Jón originally came from, and drawings of some archaeological sites
on the farmsteads where Jón *lærði* lived during his time in the east
of Iceland are shown. – The decade 1640–50 was the most fruitful period in Jón *lærði's* career as a writer. Some of his works were

written at the request of Bishop Brynjólfur Sveinsson (1605–75). Jón's main works from this period are mentioned and illustrated with a few samples of his manuscripts and some original drawings from his Natural History of Iceland. Some mention is made of Jón *lærði's* achievements as a painter and craftsman, including his work in the local church at Hjaltastaður, where he is buried alongside his wife Sigríður.

Jón lærði amid the scenes of his youth

Jón Guðmundsson (1574–1658), who already during his lifetime was given the nickname *lærði* ('the Learned'), was born in Ófeigs-fjörður in the Strandir region (Plate 2), son of a farmer, Guðmundur Hákonarson, and his wife Sæunn Indriðadóttir. As a child he got to know his maternal grandfather Indriði Ámundason, who had been a priest with Catholic roots. There was an interest in books in Jón's family and generally in the Strandir region, and a number of old manuscripts were preserved there.[146] At the manor farm Skarð, on Skarðsströnd in Breiðafjörður, Jón encountered modern printed books, including German works on botany. Jón learned to write at an early age; he copied out manuscripts which he illuminated skilfully. (Plate 3) The people of the Strandir region were largely self-sufficient. They used driftwood for building and furniture, and Jón was known for his manual skills, which included carving items from walrus tusks and whalebone. It is thought likely that the carved panels that have been preserved from the old church at Árnes in Trékyllisvík are his work (Plate 4).[147] He was an accomplished poet and became famous throughout the West Fjords after laying ghosts at Staður on Snæfjallaströnd in 1611 - 12; this no doubt played a part in the accusation of witchcraft that was levelled at him two decades later. A considerable body of poetry by Jón has survived and

---

146 Einar Gunnar Pétursson. Jón lærði – ævi og störf. Í spor Jóns lærða. Reykjavík 2013, pp. 3–36.
147 Þóra Kristjánsdóttir. Listamaðurinn Jón. Í spor Jóns lærða. Reykjavík 2013, pp. 105 12.

he is generally regarded as one of Iceland's most important poets of the 17th century.[148] In his last known poem, *Fjölmóður* ('Purple Sandpiper'), written in about 1650, he gave an account of his life in about 400 stanzas.

In 1600 Jón married Sigríður Þorleifsdóttir, an intelligent woman who stood with him through thick and thin to the end of his days. She had family connections with Skarð on Skarðsströnd where her grandfather, Klemens Ásmundsson, had been a priest. The couple went to run the farm at Stóra Fjarðarhorn in Kollafjörður in spring 1601, and a few years later Jón was working at Skarð and in the Ólafseyjar islands in Breiðafjörður, which were part of the property of Skarð (see Map I). In about 1611 the couple moved to the farm Stóra-Ávík in Trékyllisvík where they lived by fishing and farming as was the normal pattern on coastal farms (Plate 5). In stanza 197 of *Fjölmóður*, Jón says: '…hafða eg þó fyrri/formann kallazt/vel 19 ár, það vissi alþýða' ('… but earlier I had been called a boat captain for 19 years; the common people knew that'); no doubt more were added after he moved to the east of the country.

While he lived in Trékyllisvík, Jón observed the arrival of the Basque whaling ships which first appeared there in 1613 and later met members of their crews who came ashore to trade with the local people. Being curious and open by nature, he was naturally interested in these foreign whalers and the equipment they had with them. The shipwrecks of autumn 1615 and the violence that followed in their bloody aftermath, known as 'Spánverjavígin' ('Slayings of the Spaniards') marked a turning point in Jón's life. After many of the Basque survivors of the shipwrecks were killed, Jón says false allegations were made about him to the local sheriff, Ari Magnússon í Ögri (Plate 6). Ari asked him to take part in the attack on the Basques who escaped to Patreksfjörður , 'Ellegar eg skyldi/ eins og Spanir/ friðlaus vera/ og fá vel bana/ hjá hvolpum mínum/ í húsi rofnu,/ í náttmyrkri/ nístur í tóptum.' ('Otherwise, like the Spaniards, I would enjoy no peace and be killed along with my dogs in the dark, my house broken into, speared in its ruins.' *Fjölmóður*,

---

148 Ljóðasmiðurinn Jón lærði. Sýnishorn af kveðskap hans. Í spor Jóns lærða. Reykjavík 2013, pp. 233–49.

stanza 167.) Jón says he rejected this ultimatum, being unwilling to bathe himself in the blood of the Spaniards. He fled from Strandir, never to return, and moved to Snæfellsnes, leaving his possessions, including books and manuscripts, behind.

In the Introduction to his edition of Jón lærði's work *Spánverjavígin 1615*, Jónas Kristjánsson writes the following about Jón's reaction to these events::[149]

> Rit Jóns, Sönn frásaga og Fjölmóður, eru einstök að
> því, að þau eru á bandi Spánverja og draga enga fjöður
> yfir hversu hroðalega var við þá leikið. Er furða að
> fátækur bóndi skyldi þora að ganga svo í berhögg við
> æðsta valdsmann sýslunnar og aðra sem að drápu
> num höfðu staðið, enda varð honum dýr hreinskilnin;
> hann varð að hrökklast úr átthögum sínum, lenti síðan
> á flæking og lifði í basli það sem eftir var ævinnar.

(Jón's works *Sönn frásaga* and *Fjölmóður* are unique in that they take the side of the Basques and make no attempt to cover up how frightfully they were treated. It is amazing that a poor farmer should dare to cross the most powerful official in the county, and others who had taken part in the killings, in this way, and his candour cost him dearly: he had to leave his native locality, ending up as a vagrant and facing a struggle for the rest of his life.)

The *Spánverjavíg* and related events are covered in other articles in this book and so will not be given further attention here.

---

149 *Spánverjavígin 1615*. Sönn frásaga eftir Jón Guðmundsson lærða og Víkingarímur. Jónas Kristjánsson bjó til prentunar. Kaupmannahöfn 1950. Inngangur VII.

On Snæfellsnes and Suðurnes

When he first arrived on Snæfellsnes, Jón *lærði* feared that Sheriff Ari Magnússon would take his revenge on him and tried to escape from the country with an English fishing boat, but was unsuccessful. By this time he was in his middle years (aged 42), without any possessions. The slaying of the Basques received some attention at the Althingi, but no charges were brought against Jón. For the next 15 years, he and his family moved between various places in the west of Iceland and later in the Suðurnes region (see Map II). The first of these was Stapi (Arnarstapi), where he was reunited with his family and lived there for four years; the longest spell in one place was at Rif, on the northern side of the Snæfellsjökull glacier, from 1621 to 1627 (Plate 7). For further information on his life and circumstances in these places, the reader is referred to the article by Einar G. Pétursson in this book.[150] During this period Jón established contact with the bishopric at Hólar, where his son Guðmundur was accepted as a pupil. At this time Jón would probably have been busy, as before, at various occupations, including teaching and writing. His *Grænlands annáll*, which includes material on the settlement of Greenland by people from Iceland and the voyages of discovery to North America (Vínland), is believed to date from 1623.[151] In 1627, the rural dean of Snæfellsnes, Guðmundur Einarsson at Staðarstaður, wrote his *Hugrás*, in which he attacked Jón *lærði* for his poem *Fjandafæla* of 1611 and the alleged heretical ideas expressed in it, and included some general remarks about books of magic charms and formulae. He upbraided the sheriffs for not acting against sorcerers. As a result of these urgings, Jón felt insecure on Snæfellsnes and moved further south, temporarily to Akranes.

Jón and Sigríður's eldest son, Guðmundur, had in 1628 been ordained as the vicar of Hvalsnes on Miðnes on the tip of the Reykjanes peninsula in the southwest of Iceland, and Jón and his

---

150 Einar G. Pétursson, *Sönn frásaga*, in particular regarding the repercussions of the slayings, Jón's flight from Strandir, his stay on Snaefellsnes and his position there.

151 Ólafur Halldórsson. *Grænland í miðaldaritum*. Reykjavík 1978.

family were able to stay with him. After his schooling at Hólar, Guðmundur had lived abroad, including some time in Hamburg in 1623-26. After his ordination, however, Guðmundur found himself in conflict with Ólafur Pétursson, an agent of the Danish captain Holger Rosenkrantz at Bessastaðir (Plate 8). Ólafur had made advances to Helga Guðmundsdóttir, Guðmundur's fiancée, who was serving-girl at Bessastaðir. Guðmundur brought a charge against Ólafur for persecuting her with magic spells, but was himself stripped of his benefice in spring 1630 because of his charges against Ólafur. This same Ólafur accused Jón *lærði* of practising magic, citing as evidence the allegations made in *Hugrás* and a royal letter of 1617 and also the work *Bót eður viðsjá* ('Reparation or caution'), a book about magic by Jón. Jón appealed to the Althingi in 1631 and was found not guilty. Nevertheless, he was arrested by the Bessastaðir faction and sentenced to prison at a special assize session on 1 August 1631. Instead of being sent to Copenhagen for a period of imprisonment, he was ordered to move to the east of Iceland. In the course of all this the couple's two younger sons died.[152] In stanza 248 of *Fjölmóður* he says: 'Á Langanes/ til landsenda,/ skikkað var mér/ að skrölta þangað' ('To Langanes, to land's end, there I was ordered to betake myself'). It can be conjectured (see *Fjölmóður*, stanza 217) that Guðmundur, their surviving son, already moved to the east, 'til landsenda' ('to land's end')[153] in 1631 with his mother, ahead of Jón[154], who moved there separately in the winter of 1631-32. He travelled there, lame and without a horse, after Christmas, via Vopnafjörður and Hellisheiði, reaching Úthérað late in the winter (Plate 9).

---

152 Einar G. Pétursson. *Eddur it Jóns Guðmundssonar lærða I Inngangur*. Jón Guðmundsson lærði. 2. Æviferill og ritstörf. Reykjavík 1998, pp. 56–152.
153 The original manuscript of *Fjölmóður* was lost in the great fire of Copenhagen in 1728, so only copies of the text exist. Here, capital or lower-case in the word landsendi does not indicate conclusively whether this is the placename *Landsendi* or simply that the move was to a remote place.
154 Gísli Oddsson. *Bréfabók*. AM 245 4to, 77v. See also Einar G. Pétursson. Eddurit I, pp. 82–3.

At Landsendi and on Bjarnarey

Úthérað, the region flanked by the bay Héraðsflói, is where Jón lived for the rest of his life, with the exception of his trip to Copenhagen in 1636-37.[155] Five of the places he lived at are marked on Map III; all of these, with the exception of Landsendi, are known for certain. Ketilsstaðir is the outermost farm in Jökulsárhlíð on the eastern side of Hellisheiði; for a long time the farm was used as a home for the parish poor, and several tenancies belonged to it. The property of Landsendi (now abandoned) is on a piece of flat ground beneath the mountain Landsendafjall about 3 km closer to the sea. It was a tenancy of Ketilsstaðir and was occupied until about 1750, and there were sheep sheds there in the last century (Plate 10). Map IV shows the position of buildings from former times. 'Landsendi' occurs as a place-name in many parts of Iceland in similar localities, but this is the only one in the eastern quarter of the country that is known to have been inhabited in recent centuries. A couple without children were recorded as living there in the census of 1703.

Ketilsstaðir í Jökulsárhlíð was at this time the home of Hrafn (Rafn) Jónsson, who was a *lögréttumaður* (a member of the court, *lögrétta*, at the Althingi) from 1632 to 1635 and again at a later date.[156] He was acquainted with the other influential men of Fljótsdalshérað at this time such as Bjarni Oddsson (1590 - 1667), sheriff of the county of Múlaþing and the Rev. Ólafur Einarsson (c. 1573 - 1651) of Kirkjubær, paternal uncle of Gísli Oddsson, the Bishop of Skálholt at the time (Plate 11). Bishop Gísli was the brother of Árni Oddsson, who was then *lögmaður* (highest-ranking Icelandic official) in the eastern and northern parts of the country and who was already on friendly terms with Jón *lærði*, having borrowed a book of medicinal

---

155 Hjörleifur Guttormsson. Dvalarstaðir Jóns lærða á Úthéraði og í Bjarnarey. Í spor Jóns lærða. Reykjavík 2013, pp. 59–81.
156 Benedikt Gíslason frá Hofteigi. Íslenzki bóndinn. Akureyri 1950, p. 152. – Af Rafni á Ketilsstöðum. Íslenzkar þjóðsögur og sagnir VIII. Safnað hefur Sigfús Sigfússon. Reykjavík 1988, pp. 5–8. Also in Í spor Jóns lærða, pp. 261–3.

remedies from him.[157] Jón praises Bjarni, the Rev. Ólafur and other individuals in the eastern region for their kindness and favourable disposition towards him in stanzas 252 and 254 of *Fjölmóður*. I consider it likely that Jón was allowed to live at Landsendi in the years 1632 - 35. In many ways it must have been a familiar environment for him, living by the sea and being able to fish every day as at Strandir or on Snæfellsnes. When there was fishing to be had, boats could be launched from Ker, just beyond Landsendi, where there are now ruins of an old fishing shack and boathouse above the coastal bank. There are many similar sites along the coast, for example at Geldingsnes (Landsendanes) and Múlahöfn, below Ketilsstaðamúli, and also in the eastern part of Héraðsflói.[158]

In stanza 254 of *Fjölmóður*, Jón *lærði* states that Bishop Gísli and Árni *lögmaður* both came to the east of the country and had let the agent's ruling remain in force 'til þess yfirvalda urðu skipti' ('until there was a change in the authorities'). The bishop made a visitation to that part of the country in summer 1633; a new agent, Jens Söffrinsson took over a little later. In 1635, the latter declared Jón *lærði* an outlaw and ordered that he be arrested and brought before a sheriff or taken to Bessastaðir.[159] At this point Jón and Sigríður moved to the island of Bjarnarey, no doubt with the approval of the person in charge of it, Jón Ögmundsson, the vicar of Hof in Vopnafjörður. Stanza 257 of Fjölmóður says '...varð þá í útsker/ eitt að snauta' ('... had to scuttle off to a skerry'). Thus, powerful men in the east of the country once again supported Jón despite the instructions from Bessastaðir that he was to be arrested. It is likely that the couple lived on Bjarnarey until 1639 (Plate 12), i.e. until their son Guðmundur was reinstated as a minister of the church and received a position as curate at Hjaltastaður. Jón's lengthy poem *Um Gullbjarnarey* was probably composed while he was living on the island.[160] It is skilfully composed; the refrain 'Vænt er út í Bjarnarey

157   Jón Guðmundsson lærði. Tíðfordríf, 7v, *cf*. Páll Eggert Ólason. *Menn og menntir siðskiptaaldarinnar á Íslandi* IV. pp. 321–2.
158   Hjörleifur Guttormsson. Minjar um sjósókn við Héraðsflóa. *Múlaþing* 35 2008, pp. 35–67.
159   *Alþingisbækur Íslands* V (1620–1639), p. 376.
160   Svavar Sigmundsson. Vænt er út í Bjarnarey að búa.. *Mímir*, blað stúdenta í íslenzkum fræðum 1963 (2. tbl.). Also in Í spor Jóns lærða, pp.246–7.

að búa' ('Bjarnarey is a good place to live') suggests he was not unhappy there. It is a beautiful place in the summer with a lot of bird life; the sea provides plenty of fish, sharks, seals and whales. In past centuries it was frequented by fishermen from Vopnafjörður. Winters there can be severe, on the other hand, and it is an isolated place (Map V).

Father and son and their journey to Denmark

Notwithstanding the goodwill of the potentates of the east of Iceland towards Jón *lærði*, he lived under the constant shadow of his conviction and the order for his arrest. Stanza 255 of Fjölmóður indicates that his son Guðmundur made a trip abroad in 1632 or slightly later, returning with a letter from a bishop which was nevertheless ignored. Then, in summer 1636, father and son went to Copenhagen to try to have their cases sorted out by the Danish authorities. This was the only time Jón travelled outside Iceland, then aged 63. Despite certain difficulties and obstacles, which resulted in his spending some time in prison there, the trip must have broadened his horizons. For example, in Copenhagen Jón obviously met Brynjólfur Sveinsson; he was the *konrektor* of the University of Roskilde at the time and was later to become Bishop of Skálholt. This was to change Jón *lærði's* life radically later on. Also in Copenhagen, Jón met the naturalist and runic scholar Ole Worm (Plate 13), who had earlier heard reports of him as the most knowledgeable man in Iceland regarding runes.[161] At this time Worm was the vice-chancellor (*rektor*) of the University of Copenhagen. He directed the court interrogation of Jon *lærði* (referred to in the case documents as 'den lærde, eller Wisse Jon'). The court ruled that the case was to be investigated and judged anew at the Althingi; the royal letter to this effect is dated 14 May 1637. Jón returned to Iceland and appeared before a 25-man court at Þingvellir on 30 June that summer. Its finding was that the earlier sentence was to be

---

161 Worm, Ole. *Ole Worm's Correspondence with Icelanders.* Edited by Jakob Benediktsson. København 1948, pp. 225–6.

upheld 'utan kóngleg náð vilji honum meiri vægð sýna' ('unless the king's mercy is willing to show him greater indulgence'). It seemed to Jón that he was in no better a position than he had been before his trip to Denmark; nevertheless, the outcome at Bessastaðir was that instead of being transported to Denmark for punishment, he was to return to the east of Iceland.[162] It was probably while he was at Þingvellir that summer that he composed the long poem Ármannsrímur, which is preserved in four manuscripts that have subsequently been published.[163] It is known from records that Jon's wife, Sigríður, remained on Bjarnarey during the year he was in Denmark. At this time they had some ewes on the island, and by late winter she was afraid that they would die of starvation, but this did not happen.[164] The couple probably lived on the island until the spring of 1639, when various changes followed the appointment of Brynjólfur Sveinsson as Bishop of Skálholt on 15 May (Plate 14). One of the bishop's first actions was to reinstate Guðmundur Jónsson, who shortly afterwards became curate to Sigurður Mag-nússon, the vicar at Hjaltastaður. Páll Eggert Ólason[165] considers it likely that Guðmundur received a place to live at Gagnstaðahjáleiga, a little further north in the same district, on the bank of the river Selfljót, and that his parents moved there from Bjarnarey in 1639 or 1640 (Plate 15).

At Gagnstaðahjáleiga and Dalakot

It must have been a welcome change for Jón *lærði* and Sigríður to move from Bjarnarey to Útmannasveit. After almost a quarter of a century's constant upheavals and insecurity regarding the future they found

---

162 Einar G. Pétursson. *Eddurit Jóns Guðmundssonar lærða I Inngangur.* Jón Guðmundsson lærði. 2. Æviferill og ritstörf. Reykjavík 1998, pp. 56–152.
163 Íslensk rit síðari alda I. Ármannsrímur. Kaupmannahöfn 1948, pp. 1–89. Sample given in Í spor Jóns lærða, pp. 238–9.
164 Í spor Jóns lærða. Þjóðsagnabrot og munnmæli. Eftir Jóni litla lærða um föður hans og móður. Reykjavík 2013, pp. 266–7.
165 Páll Eggert Ólason. Íslenzkar æviskrár II. Guðmundur Jónsson (c. 1601–1685). Reykjavík 1949, p. 159.

themselves in a reasonably peaceful environment with the chance to concentrate on interesting tasks. They could attend church regularly at Hjaltastaður with their son, the curate. Jón's talents as a carpenter and painter were soon engaged for the renovation of the church, a task that he performed with such thoroughness that it seemed like new building and aroused the interest of visitors.[166] He carved an altarpiece with side panels and a representation of the crucifixion, dated 1643, decorated a half-panel and door-frame between the choir and the nave, including a statue of Mary and a wooden cross. In addition he built and painted a pulpit. These things remained in the church at Hjaltastaður for nearly 150 years; the statue of Mary is now in the National Museum of Iceland (Plate 16).[167] Together with these activities, Jón began writing works for the new bishop at Skálholt. Brynjólfur Sveinsson was deeply interested in ancient lore and recognized in Jón *lærði* and his contemporary Björn Jónsson of Skarðsá (1574–1655) two men who could contribute much to the understanding of the Norse pagan religion. In the final stanzas of *Fjölmóður*, preceding the 'coda', Jón sums up the transformation that occurred in his circumstances after 'að suðrið/ úr sorta birti/ með blíðum biskupi' ('the south emerged from darkness into light with a benevolent bishop'). Stanza 321 contains traces of the same sense of relief:

> Aldrei hefir fundizt
>
> í öfundarflokki,
>
> heldur hugsvalað oft
>
> og hýrt með ölmusu
>
> karl og kerlingu;
>
> krossburð undir
>
> vantar þolgæði
>
> þraut vel bera.

---

166 Þóra Kristjánsdóttir. Listamaðurinn Jón. Í spor Jóns lærða. Reykjavík 2013, pp. 105–12.
167 Hjörleifur Guttormsson. Afdrif kirkjuskreytinga Jóns lærða á Hjaltastað. Í spor Jóns lærða. Reykjavík 2013, pp. 175–96.

(Never has he stood

in the band of envy,

but often soothed

and blessed with alms

both man and woman;

constancy is needed

to carry the cross,

bear well the burden.)

Jón's first production at the bishop's behest was his *Samantektir um skilning á Eddu* ('Compilations on Understanding the Edda'), written at Gagnstaðahjáleiga in 1641. The main text of the *Edda* that Jón used was the 'Uppsala *Edda*' which he had probably copied in Copenhagen in the winter of 1636–37. Besides this copy of Snorri's *Edda*, Jón's work contains his comments on the ancient Norse beliefs and their connection with Classical paganism.[168] After this, Jón and Björn á Skarðsá were commissioned by the bishop to write a commentary on *Brynhildarljóð*, a poem found in *Völsunga saga*, which the bishop acquired in 1641, before he was given the Codex Regius manuscript of the *Edda*, where the same poem is known as *Sigurdrífumál*. Jón's commentary is often known as *Ristingar*; the full title is *Að fornu í þeirri gömlu norrænu kölluðust rúnir bæði ristingar og skrifelsi* ('In ancient times runes were known in Old Norse both as engravings and as writing'). The third work that Jón wrote during these years beside the river Selfljót was the miscellany *Tíðfordríf* ('Pastime'), which was partly a supplement to *Samantektir*. It includes a long section on 'Álfheimar eður undirheimar' ('The Elves' World, or the Underworld') and material on stones (much of which is translated) and notes on plants, Ódáinsakur and old words and proverbs. *Tíðfordríf* was completed in Gagnstaðahjáleiga on 8 May 1644.

---

168 Einar G. Pétursson. Jón lærði – Ævi og störf. Í spor Jóns lærða. Reykjavík 2013, pp. 3–36.

In 1645 Guðmundur Jónsson was appointed vicar of Berufjörður, a position he held for nearly ten years. Thus, Jón and Sigríður were obliged to find somewhere new to live, and moved from Gagnstaðahjáleiga to Dalakot, a tenancy from the farm Dalir lying a little further east in the district, now about one and a half kilometres from the new property of Hjarðarholt (Plate 17, Map VI). They may have been the last people to live at the site, which later became known by the name of Dalasel.

Probably after completing *Tíðfordríf*, Jon began work on the natural history of Iceland, the first work on the subject apart from the thirteenth-century *Konungsskuggsjá*.[169] The title is *Ein stutt undirrétting um Íslands aðskiljanlegar náttúrur* ('A Short Discourse on the Natural History of Iceland'), published in 1924 in the Islandica series.[170] Part of it is extant in Jón *lærði's* own hand, with his illustrations, and to judge from the script, his hand had started to tremble. The main part of the book is about the whales found in the seas off Iceland and Greenland, followed by sections on walruses (Plate 18), fish, birds and various invertebrates. The final sections are on minerals and metals. Another work by Jón from the same period is his *Um nokkrar grasanáttúrur* ('On the Nature of Certain Plants'). This remains unprinted. It was written at the commission of Bishop Brynjólfur, probably at Dalakot. Also extant, in a manuscript dated 1763, is *Lækningar Jóns Guðmundssonar lærða. Epter stafrófi* ('Jón Guðmundsson the Learned's Book of Medicine. Arranged Alphabetically'), and much similar material is to be found attributed to him in various manuscripts. Of Jón *lærði* as a naturalist, Steindór Steindórsson wrote:[171] 'Hann er hinn fyrsti raunverulegi náttúruskoðari meðal Íslendinga' ('He is the first real observer of nature in Iceland)', and Helgi Hallgrímsson says of him:[172] 'Jón er nú almennt talinn frumkvöðull náttúruþekkingar á Íslandi og mikilvægur heimildarmaður um hugarheim þjóðar okkar á 16. og 17. öld, um þjóðtrúna

---

169 Helgi Hallgrímsson, Náttúrufræðingurinn Jón lærði. Í spor Jóns lærða. Reykjavík 2013, pp. 83–104.
170 Halldór Hermannsson (Ed.). Jón Guðmundsson and his Natural History of Iceland. *Islandica XV.* Ithaca 1924.
171 Steindór Steindórsson. Íslenskir náttúrufræðingar. Reykjavík 1981, p. 33.
172 Helgi Hallgrímsson, Náttúrufræðingurinn Jón lærði. Í spor Jóns lærða. Reykjavík 2013, p. 101.

ekki síst' ('Jón is now generally regarded as a pioneer in the natural sciences in Iceland and an important source of information about the intellectual climate in the 16th and 17th centuries in Iceland, and not least about folk beliefs').

It was definitely at Dalakot that Jón wrote a short translation from German, *Heimshistoría Fabróníusar*, which he completed in 1647.[173] Then came his autobiographical poem *Fjölmóður*, which I have referred to often above; this was completed in 1649 and dedicated to Bishop Brynjólfur Sveinsson. It was his last known piece of writing, a fitting monument to a turbulent and eventful career. The couple lived in Dalakot for nine years, until their son Guðmundur took over the position of vicar of Hjaltastaður, where they moved and spent their final years in his care (Plate 19).

Final years at Hjaltastaður

Jón *lærði's* account of the shipwreck and slaying of the Basque sailors in 1615 is an unusually candid and objective description of the atrocities committed on the survivors of the shipwreck. He was to pay dearly for his refusal to heed the instruction to take part in the attack on them, and the result was his extraordinary career which has been traced briefly above. As far as is known, Jón and Sigríður enjoyed peace in their old age in the home of their son and daughter-in-law.

When Jón was in his eighties he started looking for a resting place in the churchyard at Hjaltastaður. Ólafur Olavius, who visited Hjaltastaður in 1776 and praised those works of Jón's that were still to be seen in the church, relates:[174]

---

173 German title: Fabronius, Hermann. *Newë Summarische Welt Historia.* Getruckt zu Schmalkalden durch Wolffgang Ketzeln 1612.

174 Ólafur Olavius. *Ferðabók* II. Steindór Steindórsson frá Hlöðum íslenzkaði. Reykjavík 1985, pp. 230–2.

Annars var mér sagt það um hann, ásamt fleiru, að
hann skömmu fyrir andlát sitt gengi fram og aftur
um kirkjugarðinn á Hjaltastað, hlustaði þar við hvert
leiði, en segði stöðugt að því búnu: „Hér eru of margir, hér er allt of ókyrrt," þar til er hann að lokum valdi
sér legstað fyrir framan kirkjudyr, því að þar sagði
hann að enginn væri grafinn, og reyndist það svo.

[Among other things about him I heard that shortly
before his death he used to walk up and down in the
churchyard at Hjaltastaður listening by each of the
graves, and after this he always said: 'There are too
many here; there's too much disturbance.' Eventually
he chose a spot in front of the church door, as he said
no one was buried there, which proved to be the case.]

A gravestone marking the couple's grave was unveiled at the
entrance to the church at Hjaltastadur on the 350th anniversary of
Jón *lærði's* death on 10 August 2008 following a conference about him
in the community centre (Plate 20). Now the idea has been mooted
of opening a scholarly centre in a former doctor's residence, built
in 1926 at the side of the church (Plate 21), to honour the memory
of this hardy and unusual achiever .

Acknowledgements

Many people have made their contribution to the material presented
here, and only a few can be credited specifically. Guðmundur Ó
Ingvarsson drew the maps; the site drawings are based on interpretations by various archaeologists and Jeffrey Cosser translated the
text as published here. As can be seen from the references, I have
drawn heavily on the book Í spor Jóns lærða (2013). Without the
work done by the contributors to that book, our knowledge of Jón
lærði's life and work would have been very much the poorer.

2. The Drangaskörð ridge, running north from Ófeigsfjörður, is a well-known feature in the district. There is plenty of drift-wood here.   HG

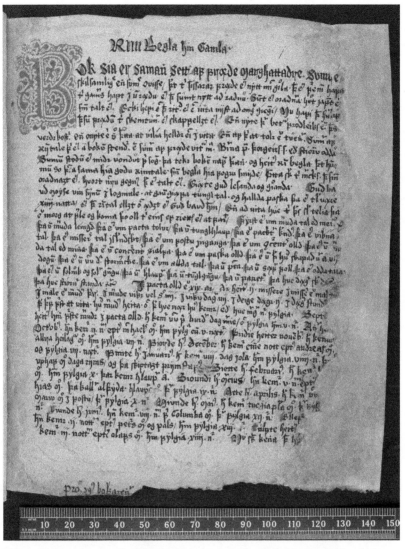

3. Rímbegla hin gamla. The beginning of Jón *lærði's* manuscript (AM
727 I 4to, 1r) dating from 1594. Rímbegla was used as the
bases of computistic works.

© Árni Magnússon Institute, Reykjavík

4. Carved panel from Árnes. It would have lain lengthways, probably as part of the roodscreen. Presumably the work of Jón *lærði*.
National Museum of Iceland

5. Trékyllisvík, seen from Reykjaneshyrna 1996. The Ávík farms are in the foreground.   HG

6. Portrait of Ari Magnússon í Ögri, with his wife Kristín, daughter of
Bishop Guðbrandur Þorláksson.

National Museum of Iceland

7. Snæfellsjökull, seen from Rif. Jón *lærði* lived in the vicinity of the glacier in the years 1617–27, first at Stapi (Arnarstapi) and then, for six years, at the tenancy of Uppsandar, above Rif.

HG

8. Holger Rosenkrantz was a Captain at Bessastaðir from 1620 to 1633. This was his family coat of arms.

Erik Rosenkrantz

9. Úthérað: the sandy shore of Héraðsflói bay and the Standandanes peninsula. In the foreground is the river Lagarfljót, the icolated farm of Húsey and the river Jökla. HG

10. Ketilsstaðir í Jökulsárhlíð. The abandoned farm Landsendi is further away beneath the mountain slope. Bjarnarey can just be seen in the distance, across from Standandanes.
HG

11. Altarpiece from the church at Kirkjubær, painted in 1648. It shows
Ólafur Einarsson of Kirkjubær í Hróarstungu with his wife
Kristín Stefánsdóttir and their 15 children, three of whom
were deceased at the time.

National Museum of Iceland

12. The island of Bjarnarey, east of Standandanes. Þerribjarg and
    Kolmúli; part of Vopnafjörður can be seen on the right.
    HG

13. Ole Worm, *rektor* (vice-chancellor) of the University of Copenhagen, was president of the committee that interrogated Jón *lærði* in spring 1637. This portrait is in the Cathedral School in Aarhus, Denmark.

Arne Frier

14. Brynjólfur Sveinsson. A pencil drawing 51 x 40 cm, by Kristín
    Þorkelsdóttir, based on a painting and written sources about
    the bishop's appearance.　　　　Kristín Þorkelsdóttir

15. The abandoned farm Gagnstöð on the northern bank of the river Selfljót. The tenancy Gagnstaðahjáleiga was in the homefield closer to the camera.   HG

16. Hjaltastaða-María. This statue of Mary from the Hjaltastaður church turned up in the collection Vídalínssafn in February 2013. Þjms. Víd. 5.

National Museum of Iceland

17. The abandoned tenancy of Dalakot in the property of Dalir in Út-
mannsveit. The circular wall enclosing the homefield is in the
centre. Inside it are the ruins of the house where Jón *lærði* lived
and was still working at his writings around 1650.

HG

18. 'Um rostunginn. Sumir kölluðu hann rosmhval, en hans skapning er þó að öllu eins og sels utan hans tvær stóru tenn og hið mikla skegg.' ('The walrus. Some call it *rosmhvalur*; its form is just like that of the seal except for its two large tusks and great beard.') Manuscript written by Jón *lærði*: S 401 XI 4to.
National and University Library of Iceland

19. Hjaltastaður farm in autumn. The mountain Beinageitarfjall (1110 m) to the east.   HG

20. The gravestone covering Jón *lærði* and his wife, Sigríður, is let into the pavement in front of the church door. Designed by Hjörleifur Stefánsson, it was laid on the 350th anniversary of Jón's death in 2008.

HG

21. Church and doctor's residence in Hjaltastaður. In the distance is
the church, dating from 1881. Closer is the doctor's residence,
designed by Guðjón Samúelsson, National Architect, in 1926;
it is now planned to convert it into a scholarly centre.
HG

Maps

I. Strandir

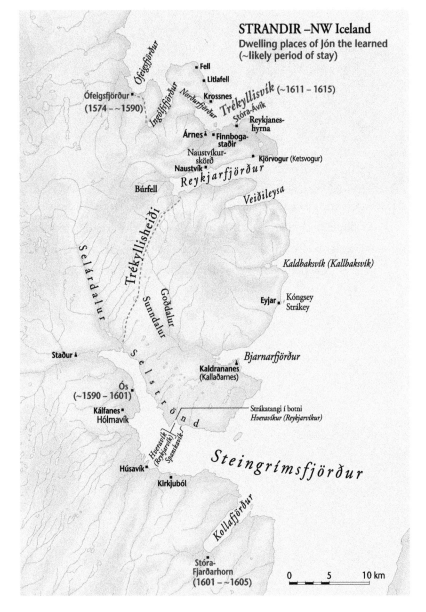

STRANDIR –NW Iceland
Dwelling places of Jón the learned
(~likely period of stay)

II. Western Iceland

WEST ICELAND

Dwelling places of Jón the learned
(~likely period of stay)

III. Úthérað

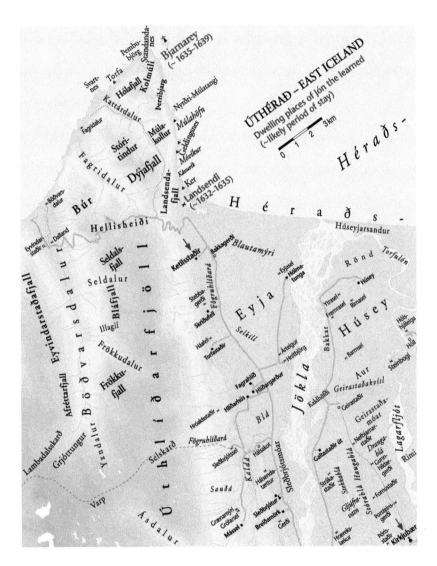

IV. Landsendi

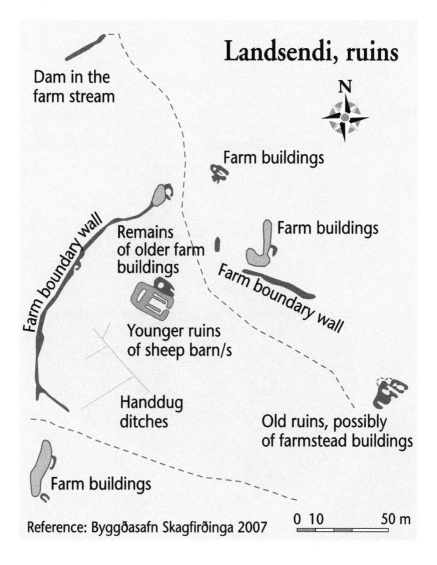

Landsendi, ruins

Dam in the
farm stream

N

Farm buildings

Farm buildings

Remains
of older farm
buildings

Farm boundary wall

Farm boundary wall

Younger ruins
of sheep barn/s

Handdug
ditches

Old ruins, possibly
of farmstead buildings

Farm buildings

Reference: Byggðasafn Skagfirðinga 2007

0 10   50 m

V. Bjarnarey

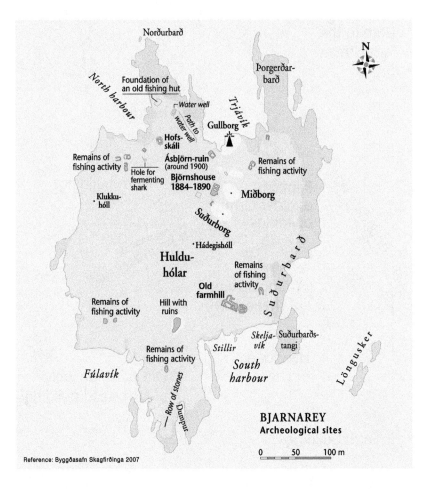

BJARNAREY
Archeological sites

Reference: Byggðasafn Skagfirðinga 2007

VI Dalakot

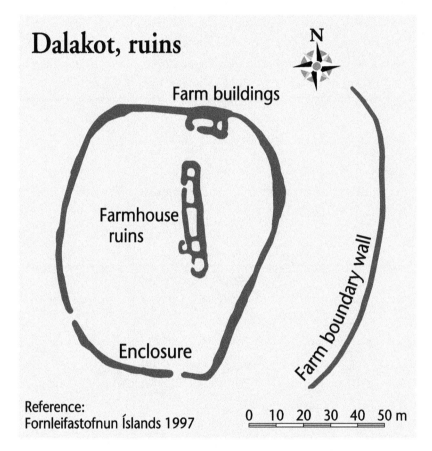

Dalakot, ruins

Farm buildings

Farmhouse ruins

Enclosure

Farm boundary wall

N

Reference:
Fornleifastofnun Íslands 1997

0 10 20 30 40 50 m

Bibliography

Alþingisbækur Íslands V (1620-1639), p. 376.

Benedikt Gíslason frá Hofteigi. Íslenzki bóndinn. Akureyri 1950, p. 152.

Íslenzkar þjóðsögur og sagnir VIII. Safnað hefur Sigfús Sigfússon. Af Rafni á Ketilsstöðum. Reykjavík 1988, pp. 5–8. Also in Í spor Jóns lærða, pp. 261–63.

Einar G. Pétursson. *Eddurit Jóns Guðmundssonar lærða I Inngangur.* Jón Guðmundsson lærði. 2. Æviferill og ritstörf. Reykjavík 1998, pp. 56-152.

Einar G. Pétursson. *Eddurit Jóns Guðmundssonar lærða I Inngangur.* Jón Guðmundsson lærði. 2. Æviferill og ritstörf. Reykjavík 1998, pp. 56-152.

Einar G. Pétursson. Sönn frásaga, in particular the repercussions, his flight from Strandir, his stay on Snaefellsnes and his position there. [See Einar's article in this conference publication]

Einar Gunnar Pétursson. Jón lærði - ævi og störf. Í spor Jóns lærða. Reykjavík 2013, pp. 3-36.

Fabronius, Hermann. *Newë Summarische Welt Historia.* Getruckt zu Schmalkalden durch Wolffgang Ketzeln 1612.

Gísli Oddsson. *Bréfabók.* AM 245 4to, bl. 77v. See also Einar G. Pétursson. Eddurit I, pp. 82-3.

Halldór Hermannsson (ritstj.). Jón Guðmundsson and his Natural History of Iceland. *Islandica XV.* Ithaca 1924.

Helgi Hallgrímsson, Náttúrufræðingurinn Jón lærði. Í spor Jóns lærða. Reykjavík 2013, pp. 83–104.

Hjörleifur Guttormsson. Afdrif kirkjuskreytinga Jóns lærða á Hjaltastað. Í spor Jóns lærða. Reykjavík 2013, pp. 175–96.

Hjörleifur Guttormsson. Dvalarstaðir Jóns lærða á Úthéraði og í Bjarnarey. Í spor Jóns lærða. Reykjavík 2013, pp. 59-81.

Hjörleifur Guttormsson. Minjar um sjósókn við Héraðsflóa. *Múlaþing* 35 2008, pp. 35-67.

Í spor Jóns lærða. Ritstjóri Hjörleifur Guttormsson. Reykjavík 2013, 350 pp. and accompanying CD.

Í spor Jóns lærða. Þjóðsagnabrot og munnmæli. Eftir Jóni litla lærða um föður hans og móður. Reykjavík 2013, pp. 266–67.

Íslensk rit síðari alda I. Ármannsrímur. Kaupmannahöfn 1948, pp. 1–89. Also in Í spor Jóns lærða, pp. 238–39.

Íslenskar Þjóðsögur og sagnir VIII. Safnað hefur Sigfús Sigfússon. Reykjavík 1988, pp. 5–8.

Jón Guðmundsson lærði. Tíðfordríf, 7v, sbr. Páll Eggert Ólason IV. pp. 321-22.

Ljóðasmiðurinn Jón lærði. *Í spor Jóns lærða*. Ritstjóri Hjörleifur Guttormsson. Reykjavík 2013, pp. 246–47.

Ljóðasmiðurinn Jón lærði. Sýnishorn af kveðskap hans. Í spor Jóns lærða. Reykjavík 2013, pp. 233-49.

Ólafur Halldórsson. *Grænland í miðaldaritum.* Reykjavík 1978.

Ólafur Olavius. *Ferðabók* II. Steindór Steindórsson frá Hlöðum íslenzkaði. Reykjavík 1985, pp. 230–32.

Páll Eggert Ólason. Íslenzkar æviskrár II. Guðmundur Jónsson (um 1601–1685). Reykjavík 1949, p. 159.

Spánverjavígin 1615. Sönn frásaga eftir Jón Guðmundsson lærða og Víkingarímur. Jónas Kristjánsson bjó til prentunar. Kaupmannahöfn 1950. Inngangur VII.

Svavar Sigmundsson. Vænt er út í Bjarnarey að búa. *Mímir, blað stúdenta í íslenzkum fræðum,* 1963 (2. tbl.).

Steindór Steindórsson. Íslenskir náttúrufræðingar. Reykjavík 1981, p. 33.

Worm, Ole. *Ole Worm's Correspondence with Icelanders.* Edited by Jakob Benediktsson. København 1948, pp. 225–26.

Þóra Kristjánsdóttir. Listamaðurinn Jón. Í spor Jóns lærða. Reykjavík 2013, pp. 105-12.

CHAPTER SIX

Violence, power relations, interests and truth. On the various accounts of the "Spánverjavíg"

Viðar Hreinsson

When discussing the so called "slayings of the Spaniards" it should be kept in mind that in the early 17th century, Basques were culturally and technologically much more advanced than the Icelanders. They had been pioneers in whaling for ages and due to their advanced technology they built large ships capable to sail to far away waters, fishing cod and hunting whales off the coasts of Newfoundland. The whale oil they provided was an important raw material in for various European industries. The Basques were thus actively participating in the rapidly developing European economy, albeit having to give way to the English and the Dutch in the struggle over power over the oceans. In addition to that, many Basques were instrumental in the Iberian conquest of the world-oceans. They were thus in the front-line in developing seafaring, contributing to the expansion of the European horizon. Basque society was developed and industrial-ized, active in international trade of the time, and the whalers who sailed to the shores of Strandir district on the Westfjords peninsula in North-West Iceland were obviously skilled and able seamen with an extensive horizon.[175]

Iceland, on the other hand, was a backward colony under Danish rule. Most of the population lived in humble sod-huts in a peasant society based on subsistence farming and fishing. The peasants were oppressed by a greedy upper class of wealthy farmers and landowners who were quite determined in fighting back all tendencies towards more mobile labor force as well as increased trade and urbanization in Iceland, in fact resisting against increased social mobility that was developing in continental Europe. After the conversion to Lutheran Protestantism in 1550, the Danish king confiscated the great wealth of the Catholic church and monasteries and the royal state power gradually strengthened. Danish monopoly trade was established in 1602 strengthening the grip further, gradually eliminating the trade with Germans and Englishmen that had been lively in the previ-ous centuries. It is however likely that some contraband trade was conducted, with English and probably Dutch merchants in the 17th century. In addition to stagnated social structures, the climate was very cold and harsh in the first decades of the 17th century, with sea ice from the north, even surrounding the country, and some sum-mers were so cold that the hay harvest and grazing failed totally. The Icelandic society had a very primitive infrastructure, lacking towns, schools, universities, domestic trade, and this weakness largely blocked for domestic initiative. The only cultural advantage the Icelanders could boast of was unusual literacy and literary activities that developed on the background of the great medieval literatures. The literary activities were at least widespread enough to keep some

---

175 William A. Douglass, *Basque Explorers in the Pacific Ocean.* (Reno: Center for Basque Studies University of Nevada, Reno), 2015, 7-12; Trausti Einarsson, *Hvalveiðar við Ísland 1600-1939.* (Reykjavík: Bókaútgáfa Menningarsjóðs) 1987, 9-35; Viola G. Miglio, "Basque Whalers in Iceland in the 17th Century: Historical Background," in *Basque Whaling in Iceland in the XVII century. Legal Organization, Cultural Exchange and Conflicts of the Basque Fisheries in the North Atlantic,* edited by Viola G. Miglio and Xabier Irujo, (Santa Barbara: Barandarian Chair of Basque Studies and Strandagaldur ses 2015) 21-52.

of the farming and fishing population fairly enlightened. At least some individuals, such as Jón Guðmundsson the learned (1574-1658) acquired self-education that fostered a broader world-view than was to be found among most of the uneducated population.

Ari Magnússon (1571-1652) was the key agent of these events in the fall of 1615. In order to establish a better understanding of his background and motives as well as the power relations in Iceland in his time, it may be useful to go a bit back in history. In the early 15th century, there were two priests, father and son, in Laufás on the eastern shore of Eyjafjörður who were renown for their magical skills, Guðbjartur flóki ("the Tangle") Ásgrímsson and his son Þorkell Guðbjartsson. They appear in a number of folktales and stories and as is common in such stories about magicians, they had the Devil in their service. The most entertaining stories are probably those penned by their colorful descendant Jón Eggertsson, a grandson of Ari Magnússon's brother, in the second half of the 17th century. He wrote a number of stories about the tricks Þorkell Guðbjartsson played upon the bishop of Hólar, but at that time, the bishops enjoyed the independence of the catholic church and used to be among the most powerful men in the country. Þorkell once visited the bishop who reprimanded him severely. His steward entered the room at that moment and behaved quite arrogantly towards Þorkell. "Take him prankster" Þorkell said, and the steward began sinking into the floor.

The bishop got frightened but Þorkell set the steward free before he disappeared. Shortly after that he returned home to Laufás. The bishop wasn't too happy with these events and decided to visit Þorkell at Laufás the following summer in order to correct him seriously. Although it was in summertime, a furious blizzard burst out when the bishop approached Laufás so he and his following got lost in the forest surrounding the farm. The bishop laid himself down under a tree and thought he would die. Then Þorkell turned the weather into sunshine and southern breeze, rescued the bishop, took him home to Laufás, warmed him up and had him served well with a bath, food and wine. And the bishop made no further attempts to reprimand Þorkell Guðbjartsson.

In reality, Þorkell Guðbjartsson (c. 1400-1483) was not only a priest, but a ruthless and greedy chieftain, actively participating in the 15th century struggles over wealth and power, in a period of weak or almost non-existent central government, when the landowning farmers consolidated their clutch on the population and hindered all attempts to develop active labor force and foreign trade. The chieftains used to ride around with large number of followers, and this period was sometimes called "sveinaöld" ("Age of Followers"). People believed strongly in magic at that time as well as the early 17th century, and Þorkell's descendants claimed that their prosperity was due to his magical skills.

Þorkell's grandson was Jón Magnússon (1480-1564), who lived in Svalbarð on the eastern shore of Eyjafjörður most of his life, married to Ragnheiður Pétursdóttir (c. 1494-1540), nicknamed Ragnheiður in the red stockings. Their descendants were called the Svalbarð clan. They had many children and all their legitimate sons became among the most powerful landowning chieftains in Iceland in the late 16th century. Sigurður Jónsson (c. 1540-1602) was a county magistrate and king's agent in Skagafjörður, Jón Jónsson (1536-1606) was a keen and ruthless lawman (lawman was the chief judicial office in the country at that time) for decades, Páll Jónsson (c. 1538-1598, better known as Staðarhóls Páll), a county magistrate, poet and a colorful character who lived in Staðarhóll and Reykhólar in West Iceland, and Magnús prúði, (Magnús the Elegant c. 1525-1591), county magistrate and a renown poet.

Magnús the Elegant lost a struggle over the profits from some sulphur mines near lake Mývatn in North Iceland and after that he moved to West Iceland. He married Ragnheiður Eggertsdóttir (1550-1642), daughter of Eggert Hannesson (c. 1516-1583), who was the most powerful chieftain and lawman in the west, extremely rich and brutal. In 1579 he was captured by some English pirates and his son in law Magnús the Elegant had to collect all silver available in the Westfjords to pay the ransom. A few years later, Eggert drank himself to death in Hamburg. Steinunn Jónsdóttir (c. 1513-after 1593), Magnús the Elegants' sister was Eggert's wife or mistress in a period. Magnús the Elegant was regarded as a rather gentle character and it was said that he healed what Eggert had damaged.[176]

The 15th century had been a ruthless age of violence and power struggles, but the situation changed somewhat after the conversion to Protestantism in 1550, that resulted in subsuming the church under the Danish royal power and the following strengthening of state power in Iceland. This development led gradually to severe restrictions of the power of the chieftains and bishops. The *chieftains thus had to adjust their conduct into accordance with the strengthening of Danish state power.*

Magnús the Elegant seems to have been a bit nostalgic and missed the turbulent Age of Followers when his ancestors gained their wealth and power. He proposed the so called Vopnadómur (sentence of arms) in 1581, a local court-sentence, in order to re-establish armed followers. In that sentence, he complained over the situation that men's arms and weapons had been destroyed a few years ago, following the order of the Danish king. He put forth a number of arguments for the necessity of organized armed forces for defense, although people of course should keep peace with foreigners as possible. But all men should provide themselves with weapons such as guns and spears, as well as tools to dig ditches and build fortresses. All capable men should be obliged to obey conscription from the authorities such as the county magistrates.[177] This sentence of arms does not seem to have been legalized, but Magnús always rode to the Alþingi (the general assembly in Þingvellir held every summer) with a large following of armed men. It is as if Magnús the Elegant aimed at restoring the Age of Followers, not fully understanding the changing times and the implications of the increasing Danish state power.

Magnús the Elegant and his wife Ragnheiður Eggertsdóttir had many children and most of their sons became county magistrates and government officials. And, as if the alliance with Eggert Hannesson wasn't enough for him, his son married a girl from the Skarð clan

---

176 Jón Þorkelsson, *Saga Magnúsar prúða*. Copenhagen: Sigurður Kristjánsson 1895
177 *Alþingisbækur Íslands* (Acta comitorum generalium Islandiæ) I, Reykjavík: Sögufélag, 1912-1914, 338-344.

that had been among the wealthiest and most powerful families in Iceland for ages. Power in Iceland was to a large extent based on these networking intermarriages between the wealthiest landowning families, whose members strengthened their power by acquiring the most important offices for the Danish royal power, thus merging the private landownership with services to the royal power.

The most powerful son of Magnús the elegant was "Ariasman" - the man behind the slayings of the Basques in 1615, Ari Magnússon of Ögur. He was extremely wealthy, greedy and physically impressive, a head taller than other men. Ari was appointed county magistrate in Strandasýsla and Ísafjarðarsýsla in 1607 and 1608 and apart from his own landownership, he was the king's steward, administering the lands confiscated from the catholic church and the monasteries. He managed at least 46 farms that in practice were an addition to his own farms, that probably amounted to some dozens. He was thus in charge of a very large part of all farms in the Westfjords. But, clearly, he was not only a wealthy landowner, county magistrate and a king's agent. He also leaned on a strong family background, being a member of the Svalbarð clan; son of Magnús the Elegant, who wanted to maintain armed forces in Iceland and a descendant of the violent chieftain-priest Þorkell Guðbjartsson the magician, which must have established a kind of a legitimization in the cultural memory, fostering the ruthlessness behind the slayings of the Basques. To sum up: Ari Magnússon was a powerful landowner and manager of land and a member of an extremely rich family, struggling to maintain and increase his wealth and power under changing circumstances, when the Danish state power was becoming ever more visible. The ruling class of landowners was in the process of redefining itself in a new situation.

The contemporary sources in Iceland about the slayings have to be evaluated against this background; actions of individuals in the context of power and interests, which inevitably affects their reliability. There are four kinds of main sources that are fundamentally different:

1. Official sources pertaining to the governance of the country, three documents from the Westfjords and closely related to Ari Magnússon, printed in the *Alþingisbækur Íslands*, as relevant documents, although there are no complete proceedings preserved from the general assembly in Þingvellir in the years 1607-1621.[178]

2. "Spönsku vísur" (Spanish Verses), a long narrative poem by rev. Ólafur Jónsson from Sandar in Dýrafjörður (1560-1627).[179]

3. Víkinga rímur (The Lay of the Vikings), probably composed not long after the events by a certain Jón Gottskálksson about whom very little is known.[180] "Rímur" are long narrative poems, usually orally performed or chanted, often composed in a highly figurative language. The singular form of the word is "ríma" but most works in the genre consist of more than one chapter, therefore the plural is used, "rímur". The length could vary from dozens to thousands of stanzas and the form was often complicated, in countless variations of the quatrain form, and the diction was often difficult).

4. Jón lærði's accounts; the prose in "A true account" and the 127 stanzas in the biographical poem Fjölmóður that deal with the slayings, including prehistory and aftermath, until Jón was forced to run away from the Strandir district.[181]

---

178 *Alþingisbækur Íslands* I, IV, Reykjavík 1912-1914: I, 309-324.
179 Ólafur Jónsson, "Spönsku vísur séra Ólafs Jónssonar á Söndum." Edited by Kári Bjarnason, in Ársrit Sögufélags Ísfirðinga 46 (2006), 119-142.
180 "Víkinga rímur." In *Spánverjavígin 1615. Sönn frásaga eftir Jón Guðmundsson lærða og Víkinga rímur,* edited by Jónas Kristjánsson. Copenhagen: Hið íslenzka fræðafélag 1950: XIV-XIX, 29-76.
181 "Sönn frásaga" In Spánverjavígin 1615. *Sönn frásaga eftir Jón Guðmundsson lærða og Víkinga rímur,* edited by Jónas Kristjánsson. Copenhagen: Hið íslenzka fræðafélag 1950: V-XIV, 1-28; Jón Guðmundsson,. "Fjölmóður. Ævidrápa Jóns Guðmundssonar lærða," in *Safn til sögu Íslands* V, edited by Páll Eggert Ólason, 3-92. Reykjavík: Hið íslenzka bókmenntafjelag 1916

Chronologically they intertwine, although in the following they will be discussed in this order. The three official documents are from the Westfjords. The first two are not accounts of the slayings as such, but simply death sentences over the shipwrecked whalers, based on a decree from the Danish king issued in the spring of 1615, but include accounts of motivations for the slayings: "Súðavíkurdómur" (The Sentence of Súðavík) dated October 8, 1615 authorized Ari Magnússon to gather forces in order to kill the Basques in Æðey, and "Mýrardómur" (The Sentence of Mýri) dated January 26 but written, signed and sealed February 27, 1616. That sentence authorized him in the same manner to go on a crusade against the Basques in Vatneyri in Patreksfjörður. At that time Jón the Learned had probably already written at least the first version of his "A True Account" since he seems to have started gathering some accounts and testimonies very soon after the slayings took place. The account may already have been in circulation at the time of Ari's unsuccessful crusade late in the winter and after refusing to go along, Jón received a death-threat from Ari or his men and ran away from Strandir in Easter, in the end of March. The last official document is a letter, "Suppliceran" from farmers and pastors in Ísafjarðarsýsla county to the Alþingi (The general assembly), written at Holt in Önundarfjörður where the prominent Sveinn Símonarson was a pastor but his wife was Ari Magnússon's cousin. The two sentences were written at the request of Ari Magnússon and probably the official letter too and all three documents are obviously statements from the power-elite in the Westfjords. Ólafur Jónsson from Sandar in Dýrafjörður was a part of that elite and composed his poem in the spring or summer, and may have based it on the Suppliceran-letter. The Víkinga rímur were probably written not long after that. The last source is Fjölmóður, Jón the Learned's auobiographical poem, or the account of his perils in life and, his recollection of the events composed in 1647, over 30 years later.

It should be mentioned here that it is well known that Ari Magnússon's actions prior to the slayings were questionable. In the first two years of the Basque whaling off the Strandir region, he had allowed the whalers to hunt and gather driftwood, received some money for it and traded with them. In the third year he turned hostile for some reasons, to some extent justified by some skirmishes between the whalers and local fishermen, and the king's decree mentioned above.[182]

The Súðavík sentence composed October 8 describes the actions of the shipwrecked Basques, stating that they violently threatened and robbed the people so that they had to run away from their homes, out to the snow and to the most distant mountain ridges, thus hindered in conducting their necessities for subsistence. The grain of truth might be that people just ran away, as the people of Steingrímsfjörður did first when the whalers came there in 1613, according to Jón the Learned in Fjölmóður,[183] and it has to be kept in mind that pirates were not uncommon at that time and people feared them.

In addition to that, the sentence contains direct lies in addition to what seems to be exaggerations, that hardly have any other purpose than serve Ari's interests since these rumors may be derived with him: "Vér greindir dómsmenn sem allir aðrir höfum spurt að fyrrnefnd þjóð hefur ekki alleinasta að leyfislausu brúkað hafnir og höndlan sína hér í landi á kóngsins lóð sem annarstaðar, heldur og í vors náðugasta herra kóngsins forboði, þar með rænt og stolið í Strandasýslu í næstu umliðin 3 ár viðum manna, nautum, sauðum og mörgum hlutum öðrum ætum og óætum, og þar með almúgann þar sama staðar margvíslega mótstaðið og til miska verið með höggum, slögum, ógn og aman, og hindran á sinni næringu. svo þetta umliðna sumar sem endrarnær, ..."[184] [We, the mentioned members of the court, have, as all others, heard that the aforementioned nation has not only without permission used harbours and trading posts on the king's land as well as other places, but also despite our merciful lord the king's prohibition, and furthermore robbed and stolen in Strandsýsla county in the last 3 years, people's timber, cattle, sheep

---

182 Már Jónsson, "Aðdragandi og ástæða Spánverjavíga haustið 1615," in Ársrit Sögufélags Ísfirðinga 46 (2006), 57-95; *Alþingisbækur Íslands* IV, Reykjavík 1920-1924: IV, 320-324.

183 Jón Guðmundsson,. "Fjölmóður, 38.

184 Már Jónsson, "Aðdragandi og ástæða Spánverjavíga haustið 1615," 82; *Alþingisbækur Íslands* IV, 311-312

and many other things, edible and inedible, and besides that, in many ways troubled and harmed the common people with beatings, blows, threats and bothering, and prevented their nourishment, this past summer as earlier, … My translation, VH]

This is referred to as hearsay, probably it was Ari's own information that he delivered to those who issued the sentence, but that contradicts other sources since it is uncontested that the whalers paid him well for license to hunt in 1613 and 1614 according to some Basque documents. Jón the Learned describes that he came for curiosity and traded with them in 1613 an did some double-dealings in 1614. But at the same time it is obvious from Fjölmóður that especially after the death of the gentle provost Ólafur Halldórsson of Staður in Steingrímsfjörður, who actually was Ari's cousin, there were some skirmishes but also some friendly relations and trade between the locals and the whalers.[185] Apparently, Ari was not a very trustworthy source. The sentence also states that the Basques did not ask for alms in God's name, which is rather strange, if people had run away already.

These descriptions based on hearsay and Ari's exaggerations are the premises for a death sentence, referring to the king's decree from the spring. The sentence also pretends to be protecting the king's interests. This is the justification of the conscription in the end of the document, that resembles Ari's father's, Magnús the Elegant's Vopnadómur (Sentence of Arms). There were severe fines for those who disobeyed and no wonder that common peasants in the neighborhood obeyed, they were probably at his mercy as tenants.[186]

In the Súðavík sentence, there is no mention of the slayings in Dýrafjörður 3 days earlier and it has been concluded that they probably didn't know about that event.[187] It is impossible to find out for sure, but right after the Basques left Strandir, a messenger was sent to Ari, who must have been on the watch, preparing for the coming of the men against whom he had turned very hostile. He might

185 Jón Guðmundsson,. "Fjölmóður, 39-41.
186 Már Jónsson, "Aðdragandi og ástæða Spánverjavíga haustið 1615," 81-83; Alþingisbækur Íslands IV, 310-313, Már 2006
187 Már Jónsson, "Aðdragandi og ástæða Spánverjavíga haustið 1615," 59

even have ordered the slayings, in the light of his power manipulations and double-dealings in general. Jón the Learned's words, that in Ögur on October 10, the news from Dýrafjörður had arrived "a few days before".[188] and it is obvious, with these self-contradictory details in mind, that the sentence can hardly be taken at face value in its description of the conduct of the Basques.

There is only a brief reference to the slayings that had already taken place in the second document, the Mýrar sentence, written in Ögur on February 27 1616, permitting or demanding a campaign in order to slay the Basques who had settled for the winter in Patreksfjörður. The text of this sentence is similar in rhetoric, style and vocabulary and ends with a conscription as well. It repeats the accusations of illegal use of the land without royal permission, stealing driftwood, as well as threat to the public and robbing from the people. It also refers to alms:

"Og nú þeir eru nauðstaddir skipbrotsmenn, leita þeir ekki öðruvísi ölmusu en svo, að þeir stela, þar ekki síður er þeim er til goda gjört og ölmusa gefin en annarstaðar, en taka víðast óbeðið lífsbjörg manna og gagnlegar kýr, eður þeir ganga svo ríkt að fólki med byssum og verjum að menn fyrir ótta sakir gefa þeim sína lífsbjörg, en sitja snauðir eftir."[189] [And now that they are shipwrecked men in distress, they do not seek alms otherwise than by stealing, no less where they have received something good or alms, but most places they take without asking people's sustenance and useful cows, or they press people so hard with weapons and armor, that people out of fear give them their sustenance but stay left in poverty. My translation, VH]

The comments on the alms contradict the Súðavík sentence, where it was stated that they didn't even ask for alms. The sentence expresses fear for acts of terror such as robbing, burning houses and killing women and children and speculates that the Basques would return for revenge if they got away alive. Everything was thus exag-

---

188 Jón Guðmundsson, "Sönn frásaga," in *1615, Spánverjavígin*. Edited by Xabier Irujo and Hólmfríður Matthíasdóttir, translated by Viola G. Miglio, Reykjavík: Mál og menning, 2015, 64/252.

189 Már Jónsson, "Aðdragandi og ástæða Spánverjavíga haustið 1615," 84-85, see also *Alþingisbækur Íslands* IV 315.

gerated in order to implement conscription, that resulted in Ari's failed crusade with 90 men, who probably would have become an easy prey for the Basques, exhausted after struggling a long distance through snow and blizzards.

The third official document, the "Suppliceran" written in Holt in Önundarfjörður June 3 1616, is similar in style but slightly different in vocabulary and might therefore be written by someone else, probably a pastor related to Ari, as for instance Reverend Sveinn Símonarson. The letter describes the alleged perils and sufferings caused by the Basques in Strandir, obviously exaggerating, stating that the Basques became increasingly obdurate and impenitent in their evil conduct. They were said to have stolen driftwood from the king and the church. The text is simply misrepresenting in stating that the slayings in Dýrafjörður were an execution in accordance with the king's decree, the instructions of the governor and a previous sentence: "En eftir kóngleg majestatis bréfi, höfuðsmannsins bífalningu og lögsömdum dómi urðu þeir slegnir hér í sýslu, sumir í Ísafirði. en sumir í Dýrafirði."[190] [Burt according to his highness' letter, the governor's order and a legally composed sentence they were killed here in this county, some in Ísafjörður, but some in Dýrafjörður. My translation, VH] No legal sentence preceded the slayings in Dýrafjörður. The letter asks the king for support and condemns those who might have helped the Basques in any way and demands punishment over them, possibly indirectly aiming at Jón the Learned, whom Ari persecuted for a few years after his escape from Strandir. The text is submissive towards the king and and portrays the "honorable" Ari Magnússon in a very favorable light as a defender of the kings' properties and interests, although it is not certain that Ari ever delivered the booty after the slayings. The documents thus seems to be a kind of an apology, intended for use in the summer assembly and Ari seems to have been defending and securing his position, well aware that that his earlier acts were highly questionable and even illegal. A year earlier, in 1614, lawman Gísli Þórðarson had to resign from his offices and pay substantial

---

190 Már Jónsson, "Aðdragandi og ástæða Spánverjavíga haustið 1615," 88, see also *Alþingisbækur Íslands* IV 318.

fines for having given an Englishman permission to catch falcons in Snæfellsnes and that must have served as a severe warning to Ari with respect to his relations to the Basques, thus explaining his sudden change in stand and attitude towards them, as writer Tapio Koivukari has pointed out in his novel *Ariasman*.[191] At the same time, Ari was perhaps testing his strength or position against the royal power as in the spring of 1615, before the slayings, when he on his own initiative fixed prices on goods and merchandise in the monopoly trade. That was a very bold act, and that year farmers and pastors from his district wrote sentences and resolutions regarding the trade.[192]

The first massacre in Dýrafjörður was executed without a preceding sentence. All three documents seem to be written in order to justify the slayings with the argument that it was for the common good and in the king's interest, that is, in reality simply to legitimize Ari Magnússon's conduct and perhaps to cover his own actions, when he received payments from the whalers in the first two years, seemingly behind the king's back. Accordingly, all those official accounts of the whalers and their activities are based on pure preconceptions, resulting in one sided hostility. The Basques are dehumanized as Torfi Tulinius has pointed out,[193] described with alienating generalizations and stereotypes, exclusively represented as a homogeneous group, as an evil nation of thieves and robbers and no mention is made of any friendly communications with the locals the three years they were in Strandir. There is no awareness of the different culture and their technological skills and abilities, but instead a total lack of a differentiating view that would have enabled the farmers to see what kind of people the Basques really were.

All three documents deliberately alienate the whalers in order to confirm and consolidate Ari Magnússons power and claim his right to do what he did. The conscription of his so-called soldiers,

---

191 Tapio Koivukari, *Ariasman: frásaga af hvalföngurum*, translated by Sigurður Karlsson. Akranes: Uppheimar 2012. See also Helgi Þorláksson, *Saga Íslands* VI, Reykjavík: Hið íslenska bókmenntafélag 255-246 and *Kongelige Allernaadigste Forordninger og aabne Breve* I, edited by Magnús Ketilsson, Hrappsey 1778, 260.
192 *Alþingisbækur Íslands* IV 262-281; Helgi Þorláksson *Saga Íslands* VI, 274.
193 Torfi Tulinius, "Voru Spánverjavígin fjöldamorð?" In Ársrit Sögufélags Ísfirðinga 46 (2006), 103-118. .

resembles Magnús the Elegant's "Vopnadómur" (Sentence of Arms), as if it was an effort to restore the old power relations of the "Sveinaöld" (Age of Followers) but at the same time securing his position under the new and strengthened Danish state power. Helgi Þorláksson may be right that the men of the Westfjords feared the danger of 80 able men going around in the starving neighborhoods stealing and robbing for a whole winter, in a period of extremely cold climate and famines.[194] But it is also possible that that Ari's so-called soldiers were offers for his manipulation, that he used exactly these arguments to instigate them for the massacres, while strengthening his own power and position. He did not have high opinions of these poor and submissive tenants of his, as is obvious in his sentence about the trade, where he addresses the common men as blind and stupid and spoilingthe trade.[195] Most likely, he was able to understand himself that since these men were exceptionally able seamen and craftsmen that would have been able to figure out means to survive in cooperation with the local population, as Jón the Learned actually suggested.

The Spanish Verses were composed by Rev. Ólafur Jónsson of Sandar (1560-1627) who was first brought up by Eggert Hannesson, but later in his youth he was in Magnús the Elegant's and his wife Ragnheiður's home so practically he was Ari Magnússon's ten years older foster brother. As a Lutheran pastor, he was thus closely connected to both realms of power, the religious and the worldly. Most of his poetry is well made, skilful craftsmanship, psalms and occasional verses. His Spanish Verses can hardly be regarded as a reliable source about the slayings, since it seems more or less to be in accordance with, or even based on the official documents, with a few details added. His point of view is the same, taking stand and condemning the whalers collectively beforehand, rhetorically calling them God's enemies terrorizing and stealing from the poor Icelanders. He exaggerates even more than the official sources, stating in that the Basques had surrounded the country for a few years (stanza 9) and stolen all the driftwood (stansza 18). No attempt is made to

194 Helgi Þorláksson *Saga Íslands* VI, 277.
195 *Alþingisbækur Íslands* IV 262-263.

understand what kind of people they were, or even their cultural background, abilities and mindset. Obviously, he was supporting his foster brother Ari Magnússon and praising him in a flattering manner, justifying his actions, primarily in the eyes of god. Both the beginning and end of the poem confirms this. Much space is spent on conventional Lutheran rhetoric about the evil, papist barbarians. The slayings are thus justified in a double sense, worldly and religiously, these official and poetic accounts are the truth of the higher powers in both domains, worldly and religious. It has been suggested that the poem was composed in 1616, and probably to some extent as an indirect response to Jón the Learned's True account. Being a religious justification, it is actually a living proof or confirmation of the Lutheran doctrine that Jón criticized bitingly in Fjölmóður, that belief only would save the souls, not the deeds, which in his view led to hypocrisy:

> Sett var orðhelgi
> í stað verka,
> gerðu það vorir
> góðu þýskir;
> mætti það duga
> að munnur pulaði
> þó að ávextir
> aldrei sæjust.[196]
> [Holiness of words
> replaced deeds,
> that was done by
> our good Germans;
> it should be enough
> that the mouth struggles
> although the fruits
> are never seen.
> [My translation, VH]

---

196 Jón Guðmundsson,. Fjölmóður, 80.

Víkinga rímur in five chapters, have been assigned to a certain Jón Gottskálksson who is assumed to have lived near Vatneyri in Patreksfjörður where the surviving Basques stayed over the winter. The poem is regarded among the worst poetry ever composed in Iceland. It is indeed clumsy in terms of grammar, idiom and the conventional imagery, to such an extent that the text is sometimes hard to understand. It is tempting to explain these faults with lack of training, that a man brought up with this kind of poetry in his ears but not having composed much until this unique occasion came up. The first two out of the five chapters are about the slayings in Dýrafjörður and Æðey and the events are somewhat mixed up. It is roughly the same story as in the Spanish verses and the official documents, and the poet takes the same general stand against the whalers, possibly because he didn't dare to draw another picture, or had not received any other account of the events. But the last three chapters are much more interesting, about the Basques who stayed in Patreksfjörður over the winter. There are a few stanzas about their seemingly friendly dealings with Ari Magnússon's mother, Ragnheiður Eggertsdóttir in Sauðlauksdalur, although the poet states that she provided them with supplies out of fear. There is also an account of Ari's failed winter trip with 90 men to Patreksfjörður and the capturing of the English ships on which the Basques eventually escaped. The poem is also interesting because there are, perhaps unintentionally, glimpses of decent behavior among the much hated strangers, they tried to be polite at least once. The obscure Jón Gottskálksson who composed the Víkinga rímur seems to have been a peasant living in Patreksfjörður. He mentioned that his father was taken prisoner and bound for a while by the Basques, so it is natural that he was irritated towards the intruders into the peaceful life in Patreksfjörður, but his hostility is not nearly as profoundly condemning and alienating as in Spanish Verses and the official documents. It is tempting to regard the Víkingarímur as the common peasant's view, uninfluenced by Ari Magnússon.

Jón the learned's accounts are fundamentally different from these sources in many ways. The "A True Account" is apparently written with the sole aim to tell the story as truthfully as possible. Jón seems however not to have realized the consequences, that his life would be threatened and that he would have to escape from Strandir. He had been on friendly terms with Ari Magnússon and the Svalbarð clan, and the Skarð clan as well, most likely conducting some scholarly work for them. He began to write "A True Account" soon after the events took place, first describing the prehistory, that he already knew, and then gathering accounts from those who were present at the slayings, among others the dubious pastor Jón Grímsson of Árnes, who's part in the story is not very flattering. Then there are around 127 stanzas about the slayings and the aftermath in his poem Fjölmóður, traditionally regarded as an autobiographical poem.

The main difference lies in the perspective, or point of view. While the other sources generalize and alienate the whalers as a single group, a hostile nation of thieves and criminals, Jón is personal. He had acquainted himself with many of the whalers and become friends with them, he describes their characters and behavior. He describes in details the slayings of men he knew personally and describes their reactions according to his knowledge of them. And he understood the religious relics that the pilot Peter had, while the others just thought this was some catholic sorcery. Jón's works are the only sources whose author had a direct contact with the Basques.[197] He does not try to conceal the behavior of the few rowdy guys among them, such as some thefts of sheep. He also has a very critical stand towards the Icelandic authorities, and mentions in the preface to one of the two existing versions of "A True account" that some of those who participated in the slayings, five of his neighbors and rev. Jón Grímsson, were submissive to Ari Magnússon and three of them being his tenants, thus underlining the aspect of social and political power. This reveals his ability to observe the situation critically in a larger context.

His detailed descriptions that obviously are based on a very keen observation, seriously question the accounts of the official

197 Magnús Rafnsson "Cultural Exchange and Socialization in the Westfjords," in *Basque Whaling in Iceland in the XVII century. Legal Organization, Cultural Exchange and Conflicts of the Basque Fisheries in the North Atlantic*, edited by Viola G. Miglio and Xabier Irujo. Santa Barbara: Barandarian Chair of Basque Studies and Strandagaldur ses 2015:297

documents and the Spanish Verses, and even proves that the descriptions are blunt exaggerations or lies. Jón's descriptions reveal complicated relations between peoples and the Icelanders' mildly speaking primitive manners and poor understanding of trade. There had been harsh climate and famines in the preceding years, so the people's situation was poor. The Basques were generous and gave much whale meat to the people, but demanded very little in return, more like token of trade rather than real trading, but Ari Magnússon had obviously turned hostile that summer of 1615:

"Nú veiddu þeir fyrir sjálfa sig ellefu stóra hvali, en svo tókst til að þeir járnuðu og misstu aðra ellefu, og var jafnan þvesti til reiðu hverjum sem vildi. En það mislíkaði þeim stórum ef menn forsmáðu að koma til þvestisskurðar áður en þau spilltust, því að fáir voru héraðsmenn og þar með félausir eftir soddan fellir. En þessir Spánskir vildu heldur nokkuð hafa en alls ekkert og þó ekki væri utan ein smjörskaka lítil, einir vettlingar, leggjabönd, hundur eða hvelpur. Fyrir sérhvört þetta þá fékk maður þvesti upp á sinn hest eða bát, hvert sem hann hafði. Sumir þorðu ekki til þeirra að fara vegna bréfa og skipanar yfirvaldsins, bóndans Ara Magnússonar, hvers bréf ennþá til sýnis eru. Sumir forðuðust það ekki, en hvör þar hafði einn sauð til sölu, nokkuð meira af einu og öðru, mátti stóran ávinning hafa, sem sönn raun bar vitni þar sem þá síldrekakálfana keyptu."

[It so happened that they hunted for themselves 11 big whales, and they harpooned but lost another 11. Lean whale meat was available for anyone that wanted it, and they really disliked it if people did not show up for the cutting of the meat before it was spoiled.. But the people in the district were few and moreover they had no money after that great winter famine. Still the Spaniards would rather have had something than nothing at all, had it been just a little pat of butter or mittens, sock garters, a dog or a puppy; for whatever the people offered, in return they got lean whale meat to down their horse completely or fill up their boat, whichever they had come with. Some people dared not to go to them because of the letters and orders not to do so from the authorities represented by Ari Magnússon the landowner, letters which can still be seen. Some though paid no heed, and whoever had a sheep or some other thing to sell, whatever it was, would find great gain from the bartering, which is true and can be proved by those who bought Rorqual calves.][198]

In Fjölmóður, Jón describes how Ari traded with them in the two previous years, and in other documents it is confirmed that he sold them permission to hunt whales and collect driftwood.[199] The locals traded with them more or less daily and some of them stole from them and cheated on them intentionally. Jón describes in details the difference in the Icelanders' behavior to the captains, that they hardly ever paid anything to Martin Villafranca, which explains why he threatened pastor Jón Grímsson the day before the shipwreck, he simply wanted to get some payment for whale products that pastor Jón had received. This description reveals the relations:

"Þennan sama áðurgreindan miðvikudag sem þeir Pétur og Stephan komu heim til sín frá Marteins skipi, velglaðir, vorum vér nokkrir viðstaddir við þeirra tjöld og búðir. Þá sagði Pétur og Luys, að nú hefði capitain Marteinn af stóra skipinu viljað finna prest um forlíkun hvals, bæði fyrir þann sem hann hefði misst af hvalshausnum í myrkrinu og svo fyrir sinn part, sem hann hefði jafnan vísitandi keypt og aldrei sér launað né þakkað, þar með hefði hann ekki eitt sinn neinu viljað við sig kaupa í allt sumar. Hirði eg ekki gjör frágreina. En það var sumra vor sveitarmanna setningur og áform, bæði í fyrrasumar og nú, að taka frá þeim og villa hvað menn treystu sér, en sumir vildu þar um grandvarir vera."

[Some of us were present at their tents and camp on the same Wednesday we mentioned before, when Pedro and Esteban came back happy from Martín's ship. Then Pedro and Luis said that at that point Martín, the captain of the big ship, would have wanted to visit the pastor to get compensation for the whales, both the one part of whose head went missing in the dark and for the one he had bought, but never paid or gave thanks for. Moreover, no one had wanted to barter with him that summer. I don't want to waste more words on this. But some of the men from our district

198 Jón Guðmundsson, "Sönn frásaga," in *1615, Spánverjavígin.* Edited by Xabier Irujo and Hólmfríður Matthíasdóttir, translated by Viola G. Miglio, Reykjavík: Mál og menning, 2015, 56/239.
199 Jón Guðmundsson,. Fjölmóður, 39. *Alþingisbækur Íslands* IV 322.

had decided that it would be a good idea to steal from them both last year and this summer, or make things disappear from them as much as they dared to do, however others wanted to act in all correctness with them.[200]

From Jón's descriptions, it is obvious that some ignorant locals spoiled the mainly peaceful relations and clear that the descriptions in the official documents and the Spanish verses are exaggerations in the interest of Ari Magnússon, whose power is overwhelming. After the shipwreck, Jón wanted to take some of the whalers to his house, obviously his idea was that they could be divided between farms in the district to some extent. "Þeir sjálfir hefðu getað nokkuð fyrir sér haft" [Perhaps they could have worked a little for their keep][201] he said, fully aware how able the men were. Many of the Basques wanted to stay, but reverend Jón of Árnes and Jón Þórðarson of Kesvogskot urged them to go to the Westfjords and told them of a ship in Dynjandi, although Jón the Learnded thought this was dangerous and that the ship was no good. "Margir af undirmönnum eður bartskerar og skipsdrengir báðu strengilega að meðtaka sig í einhvörn máta, þegar þeir aðeins héldi lífinu, en það þorði enginn að láta undirtakast, mest sakir yfirvaldsins [Ari Magnússon]. Margt þá tóku þeir í mál, þó ei yrði af, einnin að fara á fátæki eða að senda til bóndans [Ari Magnússon] Það varð nú hér af drjúgast sem hinir dýrari ráðlögðu, að þeir færi á öllum bátum sem til voru og svo norður fyrir Strandir sem leið liggur, og voru þá í búningi þennan föstudag." [Many of the subordinates, whale cutters and shipmates, begged repeatedly to be taken in so that they could at least remain alive, but no one dared to do that because of the authority [i.e. Ari]. They considered many ideas, although eventually nothing came of them, including the idea that poor people are the responsibility of the on whose land they find themselves, and that Ari would have to take care of them. It was then decided to do what those more powerful had suggested, that they would go in all their boats that were still undamaged north along the Strandir district directly, and they were preparing for such a trip that Friday.][202]

200 Jón Guðmundsson, "Sönn frásaga," in *1615, Spánverjavígin*, 57-58/243-244.
201 Jón Guðmundsson, "Sönn frásaga," in *1615, Spánverjavígin*, 59/245.
202 Jón Guðmundsson, "Sönn frásaga," in *1615, Spánverjavígin*, 60/246.

Obviously, the powerful Ari Magnússon was very present in his absence and the most prominent locals had the upper hand about sending them away, maybe to get them closer to Ari and his power. According to Jón, they had even discussed the possibility to go on alms, which underlines further the exaggerations of the official documents. As soon as the Basques had left, a man was sent to Ari, so he was obviously prepared, and there was ample time to send messages to the coastline in order to prepare for the shipwrecked travelers, whether the slayings in Dýrafjörður was ordered by him or not. And according to Jón, the people in Ögur learned about the slayings in Dýrafjörður a few days before October 10, that is, Ari must have received news about it when the Súðavík sentence was approved.

Jón's exceptionally careful work and critical use of sources indicate that his account is very reliable, contrary to the rhetorical and alienating accounts in the other sources. Ari sent for men to Árneshreppur for the conscription, but then Jón was away, thus excused from not taking part. He collected testimonies and used a number of written documents as well, that are not preserved. He is careful not to mention common peasants who took part, and sometimes he relies on written accounts: "Er það skafið úr línu hvör þá til liðs kom" [The names of the men who attacked him were erased from the manuscript line] he says,[203] which indicates some form for censorship. It is not known for certain when in the winter Jón wrote the account in two versions, but it must have been a severe blow for Ari. Jón's accounts show that some documents were deliberately destroyed, as they could put Ari in an unfavorable light.

The descriptions in Fjölmóður are somewhat less personal but, on the other hand, he observes the events in a larger perspective, since he could, 30 years later, see the overall picture in a clearer light. Differences in single details are small, which indicates that Jón's memory was astonishingly good. He mentions that Ari's mother, Ragnheiður Eggertsdóttir in Sauðlauksdalur and her son and Ari's brother Björn received the Basques in Patreksfjörður well with alms. Fjölmóður also gives an account of the aftermath. According to

---

203 Jón Guðmundsson, "Sönn frásaga," in *1615, Spánverjavígin*, 65/253.

the poem, Ari threatened to have Jón killed if he wouldn't join the army after the second conscription for the Patreksfjörður crusade. Jón refused to join the crusade and wrote Ari a letter, possibly the "A True Account" or a version of it. Ari became furious, and wrote a wrathful letter back and then Jón ran away to Snæfellsnes peninsula in the Easter 1616, lost much of his belongings but the family survived. He was persecuted for years after, at the initiative of Ari, but enjoyed the protection of powerful men in Snæfellsnes. He was obviously a serious threat to Ari and the Svalbard clan, the power-elite of the Westfjords. And in 1617, some prominent men from that region wrote a statement declaring that Jón was a sly and deceitful man and that he had left the district because of his lies, dishonesty, stupid talking and attempts to increase discord in the neighborhood.[204] But he enjoyed the support of powerful men and it is even likely that he was in possession of some letters or documents that would prove Ari's illegal actions. In Fjölmóður he hints at letters or documents that he promised bishop Guðbrandur Þorláksson not to show anyone, if Guðbrandur would take Jón's son Guðmundur into the latin school at Hólar. But that is another story.

We know that this was a violent period in history, and at that time human life was not valued in the same way as is pretended nowadays, and brutality in warfare was common just as it is today. This was the age of hateful religious wars and the witchcraft craze and in the light of that, the cruelty of the slayings is to some extent understandable but hardly justifiable, even taking the king's decree into account. But the account of Jón lærði proves that there also existed ideas of human compassion and mercy. In order to express the truth and in name of humanity he put himself in great danger by writing "A True Account" for which he was persecuted. It was the comon man's defense of humanity against the dehumanizing stereotypes produced by the power-elites and their humble servants. If we didn't have Jón's accounts now, the only accounts of the slayings would be of heroic Icelanders killing brutal Spanish intruders, villains and thieves.

---

204 Guðmundur Einarsson, *Hugrás*, Lbs 494 8vo, 92r.

Bibliography

Alþingisbækur Íslands (Acta comitorum generalium Islandiæ) I, V. Reykjavík: Sögufélag, 1912-1914, 1920-1924.

Douglass, William A. *Basque Explorers in the Pacific Ocean.* Reno: Center for Basque Studies University of Nevada, Reno, 2015.

Einarsson, Guðmundur. "Hugrás," a manuscript at the National and University Library of Iceland, Lbs 494 8vo.

Einarsson, Trausti. *Hvalveiðar við Ísland 1600-1939.* Reykjavík: Bókaútgáfa Menningarsjóðs 1987.

Guðmundsson, Jón. "Sönn frásaga." In *Spánverjavígin 1615. Sönn frásaga eftir Jón Guðmundsson lærða og Víkinga rímur,* edited by Jónas Kristjánsson. Copenhagen: Hið íslenzka fræðafélag 1950: V-XIV, 1-28.

Guðmundsson, Jón. "Sönn frásaga," in *1615, Spánverjavígin.* Edited by Xabier Irujo and Hólmfríður Matthíasdóttir, 51-71 / 235-261. Reykjavík: Mál og menning, 2015.

Guðmundsson, Jón. "Fjölmóður. Ævidrápa Jóns Guðmundssonar lærða," in *Safn til sögu Íslands* V edited by Páll Eggert Ólason, 3-92. Reykjavík: Hið íslenzka bókmenntafjelag 1916.

Jónsson, Már. "Aðdragandi og ástæða Spánverjavíga haustið 1615," in *Ársrit Sögufélags Ísfirðinga* 46 (2006), 57-95.

Jónsson, Ólafur. "Spönsku vísur séra Ólafs Jónssonar á Söndum." Edited by Kári Bjarnason, in *Ársrit Sögufélags Ísfirðinga* 46 (2006), 119-142.

Koivukari, Tapio. *Ariasman: frásaga af hvalföngurum.* Translated by Sigurður Karlsson. Akranes: Uppheimar 2012.

Kongelige Allernaadigste Forordninger og aabne Breve I, edited by Magnús Ketilsson, Hrappsey 1778, 260.

Miglio, Viola G. "Basque Whalers in Iceland in the 17th Century: Historical Background," in *Basque Whaling in Iceland in the XVII century. Legal Organization, Cultural Exchange andConflicts of the*

Basque Fisheries in the North Atlantic, edited by Viola G. Miglio and Xabier Irujo, 21-52. Santa Barbara: Barandarian Chair of Basque Studies and Strandagaldur ses 2015.

Rafnsson, Magnús. "Cultural Exchange and Socialization in the Westfjords," in *Basque Whaling in Iceland in the XVII century. Legal Organization, Cultural Exchange andConflicts of the Basque Fisheries in the North Atlantic*, edited by Viola G. Miglio and Xabier Irujo, 293-318. Santa Barbara: Barandarian Chair of Basque Studies and Strandagaldur ses 2015.

Tulinius, Torfi. "Voru Spánverjavígin fjöldamorð?" In in *Ársrit Sögufélags Ísfirðinga* 46 (2006), 103-118.

"Víkinga rímur." In *Spánverjavígin 1615. Sönn frásaga eftir Jón Guðmundsson lærða og Víkinga rímur*, edited by Jónas Kristjánsson. Copenhagen: Hið íslenzka fræðafélag 1950: XIV-XIX, 29-76.

Þorkelsson. Jón. *Saga Magnúsar prúða*. Copenhagen: Sigurður Kristjánsson 1895.

Þorláksson, Helgi. *Saga Íslands* I. Reykjavík: Hið íslenska bókmenntafélag 2003.

CHAPTER SEVEN

The Fate of the First Icelandic Journalist, Jón the learned. Interaction of man and society in the era of sorcery-fear and premature justice in the first half of the 17th century.

Ólína Kjerulf Þorvarðardóttir

Ísafjarðardjúp, the "blue bay" of West Fjords, is an area of magnificent nature, with its fishing waters and sources of valuable sea-products, an area not only rich of clear colors and sounds but of culture and history as well. There is nothing like sailing on a boat inwards Ísafjarðardjúp in a good weather, having the snow-white *Snæfjallaströnd* (Snowy-Beach) on one hand and the mountain *Hest-fjall* (Horse-Mountain) ahead. On such a day it is hard to picture the beautiful surrounding of Ísafjarðardjúp as the scene of a cruel massacre – the only one of its kind ever committed in Iceland.

Nevertheless this was the case in 1615 at Æðey (Eider-Island) and *Sandeyri* (Sandbank), when the flashes of an enormous thunderstorm lightened up the sky as well as the cruel scenery where the county's magistrate, Ari Magnússon in Ögur and his men, killed 18 shipwrecked whale-hunters from the Basque Country – 13 others had been killed in *Dýrafjörður,* a fjord nearby, a day or two before. These two events which cost the lives of 31 Basque whalers have ever since been referred to as "The Slaying of the Spaniards" *(Spánverjavígin).* In the early 17th century geographical knowledge was not as widespread among the Icelandic public as in later times, so the Icelanders did not distinguish between Basque Country and Spain, no more than they did between Turkey and Algeria (as the invasion of Algerian pirates in several Icelandic villages 1627 has been referred to as *Tyrkjaránið,* i.e. invasion of Turks, for example).

In general one must admit – in spite of the area's beauty and peaceful appearance – that the closer to West Fjords the harsher, crueler and more obscure the events of the ancient stories become. This is the case of the Sagas – and this was definitely the case in 1615.

The West Fjords have a reputation of magic and witchcraft. In this area the Icelandic witch-trials of the 17th century were the most frequent ones. Fourteen of the 21 Icelanders convicted as witches and burnt at the stake were from the West Fjords, nine of them were tried, convicted and executed by the District Court – five were executed by the Higher Court at Althingi. Therefore the 17th century West Fjords can be considered to have been an unsafe place to stay in for some.[205]

But the area of West Fjords also has it's writers, poets, scientists and artists – such as for example Jón Guðmundsson "lærði" (Jón the learned), a man with a remarkable life-story, a man of remarkable skills and intellect, but at the same time a powerless man with no formal status in life and therefore without the possibility to enhance or secure his own life condition. Let us now turn to the incident that changed entirely the life of this man for the worse: The so-called Slaying of the Spaniards when the county's magistrate Ari Magnússon in Ögur had 18 Basque whale-hunters brutally killed in one night.[206]

---

205 Ólína [Kjerulf] Þorvarðardóttir 2000: Brennuöldin. Háskólaútgáfan. Reykjavík.
206 Jónas Kristjánsson 1950: Spánverjavígin 1615, Reykjavík.

A Massacre in a Thunderstorm

How could that happen? Until this very day we still wonder. By the time of this event people had difficulties comprehending the cause and the meaning of what actually took place in Æðey, *Sandeyri* and *Dýrafjörður*. One of the few who apparently had the guts to stand up against the county's magistrate, and describe this massacre as it had happened, was Jón the learned. In his "True Account of the Shipwrecks and Slayings of the Spaniards" (*Sönn frásaga af spænskra manna skipbrotum og slagi*) Jón describes how the weaponless men were slaughtered, how the magistrate's promise of mercy in return for surrender was betrayed, and how some of the men were molested and humiliated not only before death but *post mortem* as well.[207] The wild fury of Ari's men and the frenzy while the massacre took place is not so hard to imagine though, especially when one thinks of the raging thunderstorm this particular night that may have increased the aggression and wrath of the men involved – none like it has ever raged in our country. Some have suggested that the life-loss this particular night had never been the intention of Ari the magistrate, but that he lost control over his troop.[208] Whether that was the case or not we don't know. The result is what matters, the life-loss of 18 men, and in a way also a loss of one local man's livelihood and his possibility of future prosperity. That man was Jón the learned.

Jón's "True Account" was the only document for ages ever written in the Basque whalers' defense. By his writing, Jón stirred up the wrath and anger of the county magistrate Ari Magnússon in Ögur, who of course did not like the way Jón described the mercy-less killings of the Basques – Ari most likely claiming this to be a justifiable deed while Jón saw it as an unjustifiable crime. Ari's anger was in fact a big threat to Jón the learned. Therefore Jón dared not to stay within the sphere of Ari's authority, so he fled from West Fjords during Easter 1616, leaving behind his wife and children. Later Jón was persecuted for witchcraft, convicted and expelled as

---

207   Jónas Kristjánsson 1950: Spánverjavígin 1615.
208   Árni Arnarson 1996: Náttvíg Íslands II, Lesbók Morgunblaðsins, p.10.

a witch in 1631.[209] In general Jón was defamed by powerful men as can be seen by the testimony of 16 men from West Fjords, cited by the referent Guðmundur Einarsson in his thesis *Hugrás*:

> Saying that J[ón] G[ud]M[undsson] is a cunning man and an unreliable one, and that he had disserted his district away from his unfair dealings, lies, dishonesty and guilty consciousness because how often he had spoken nonsense, gossip and evil speeches, and therefore caused disagreement and enmity between neighbors. (Translated and inserted by ÓKÞ)

> *So látande, ad Sagdur J[ón] G[ud]M[undsson] sie slægur madur og óhollur, og hafe þadann ur Sveitum rymt, fyrer óskil, lygar, órádvendne, og sakbitna samvitsku, af þvi ad farid hafe optlega med bulldur, mas, rugl og vondar rædur, og aukid so ófrid Sudurþycke og tvidrægne manna a mille.*[210]

In spite of being expelled from society – first by the district court at Bessastaðir 1631, later at Althingi 1637[211] – Jón Guðmundsson had no choice other than to stay in Iceland, where he lived as an outlaw, dependent on the mercy of his friends and supporters, for the rest of his life. But who was this man in fact? Was he one of a kind? Did he ever have a chance to "fit in" into his own society in the era of sorcery-fear and premature justice in the first half of the 17th century?

A Misunderstood Man

Jón the learned was a man of common origin. A poor and powerless man. He never had the opportunity to gain a formal education, but he earned his nickname as a self-educated scholar in his own right. Jón's scientific interest

---

209   Alþingisbækur Íslands V, p. 376, 483-484.
210   Lbs. 494 8vo (manuscript), p. 92r-v – insertion ÓKÞ.
211   Alþingisbækur Íslands V, p. 484.

may have been due to the 17th century's increasing interest for secular science such as ancient literature and science of nature for example. Educated men such as Arngrímur lærði Jónsson (1568-1648), Þorlákur Skúlason bishop at Hólar (1597-1656) and Brynjólfur Sveinsson bishop at Skálholt were all role models that without doubt increased scientific interest in Iceland. The humanism (later secularism) was a global trend at the time – driven by the earlier discoveries of Copernicus (1473-1543) and Galileo (1564-1642) and may have had its influence in Iceland, even on a plain common man such as Jón the learned – who lived at the brink of two centuries, representing them both.

Jón Guðmundsson was a misunderstood man. He was misunderstood by his fellow countrymen, and by the authorities as well, as has repeatedly been stated:

> ... and because of his knowledge of runes and similar alphabets, also the Edda poetry, being cocky and chatty as he was, he managed to get in contact with the highly educated scholar Dr. Olaf Worm and others whom he convinced that he had not done anything illegal, but only exercised natural and legal methods wherefore – due to envy and ignorance of the Icelanders – he had to suffer such a great injustice that he had to flee as a refuge and appeal his case to his majesty's graciousness. (Transl. ÓKÞ)
>
> *... og af því kunnugur var í rúnum og þessháttar stafrófi, sömuleiðis Eddukenningum og þar með raupsamur og skrafinn, þá gat hann komið sér í tal við þann hálærða mann Dr. Olaf Worm og fleiri og talað svo fyrir þeim, það þeir meintu hann engar óleyfilegar konstir, heldur náttúrlegar og leyfilegar hefði um hönd haft, en af öfund og þekkingsrleysi fólks hér í landi, liðið svo stóran órétt, að flýja hefði orðið til kongl. náðar.*[212]

---

212 Jón Halldórsson 1911-1915: Biskupasögur, p. 87.

This description of Jón's own interpretation of his case indicates that the uneducated common people of 17th century Iceland did not understand what his studies were about. He was believed to be a "power-poet" (*kraftaskáld*), that is an Icelandic concept frequently used in earlier times meaning someone who has such a high poetical spirit that his or her poems turn out as spells. He was also believed to be a healer, according to his own statements cited by referent Guðmundur Einarsson in his thesis *Hugrás* where Jón is said to have …

> … cured people of illness by laying of hands, chanting and praying, and that this service of his was as well appreciated as a help from the heavenly father himself … (Transl. ÓKÞ)
>
> … *hendur yfer sjuka lagt, med lesnijngum og bænum og þuilijk sijn þiónustugioörd hafe j þann tijma so þöckud verid, so sem hiálp og adstod af himnafodurnum sialfum send.*[213]

The Healer and the Ghost-Buster

When Jón Guðmundsson was convicted for witchcraft in 1631 the District Court at Bessastaðir took into consideration a manuscript with the title *Bót eður viðsjá við illu ákasti* (Cure or Precaution against Evil Assault). The manuscript was described as …

> … a leaflet and a few pages that the defamed man Jón Guðmundsson admitted to have written, wherein there were a few points called cure or precaution against evil assault: 1. Fire, 2. Bleeding, 3. Weapons, 4. Physical desires, 5. Madness, 6. Against assault of elves, 7. False judgements, 8. Temptations of the evil, 9. Protection against enemies and hatred of others, 10. Anger management, 11. Scaring off enemies, 12. To facilitate child-birth, 13. A verse against fall, 14. To avoid shipwrecking, 15. A verse to avoid fire, 16. Against theft,

---

213 Lbs 404 8vo (manuscript), p. 92r.

17. Against water damage, 18. Against off-springs of humans and creatures, 19. Against hallucinations, 20. Against madness, 21. A triumph-verse for war, 22. To make a weapon blunt, 23. Names of Christ-fingers, 24. To drive foxes away, 25. Cure for damage of fire, water and weapons if faith follows, 26. Blessing of victory in the morning, 27. Against the storms of sea, 28. Against marine ghosts, 29. Carving against the jaundice, 30. Several advice to prevent bleeding ... (Transl. ÓKÞ)

... kver og nokkur blöð, sem sá ryktaði maður Jón Guðmunds-son [...] meðkenndi sig skrifað hafa, hvar inni eð stóðu nokkrir punktar og kallaðir bót eður viðsjá við illu ákasti: 1. Eldsgangi, 2. Blóðrás, 3. Vopnum, 4. Líkamsgirndum, 5. Vitfirringu, 6. Álfagangi, 7. Röngum dómi, 8. Fjanda freistni, 9. Hlífð á móti óvinum og annara hatri, 10. Að stilla reiði, 11. Óvini hrædda að gera, 12. Jóðsjúra kvenna frelsi, 13. Vers fyrir falli, 14. Að hlífa skipsskaða, 15. Vers að hlífa eldsvoða, 16. Við stuldi, 17. Við vatnsskaða, 18. Við afbendi manna og kvikinda, 19. Við ofsjónum, 20. Við æði, 21. Sigurvers í stríði, 22. Að deyfa vopnabit, 23. Kristi fingra nöfn, 24. Að burt stefna refum, 25. Bót við elds-, vatns—og vopnaskaða, ef trúin fylgir 26. Sigursign-ing a morgna, 27. Við sjávarstormi, 28. Við sjódraugagangi, 29. Ristingar fyrir gulusótt, útsótt, matleiða, hósta, kláða og höfuðverk, 30. Blóðstemmur aðskiljanlegar og annað fleira ...[214]

This particular leaflet, long lost but remembered because of the written verdict, turned out to be the evidence proofing Jón Guð-mundsson's guilt. Apparently none of the 30 points stated above have the purpose of making harm of any kind, on the contrary all the advice are meant to heal or prevent damage or harm. The context of the leaflet proofs on the other hand the folk belief and superstition of 17th century Iceland, even obvious in the writings of priests and bishops of that time, such as bishop Oddur Einarsson (1559-1630) for example[215] and his son Gísli Oddsson (1593-1658)

---

214 Alþingisbækur Íslands V, 483-84.
215 Oddur Einarsson 1971: Íslandslýsing.

as well.[216] Surely Jón Guðmundsson was superstitious man, but so were most of his fellow countrymen in his lifetime. One proof of that is the pure fact that last but not least Jón the learned was a ghost-buster, hired to bust the famous Snowy-Mountain Ghost (*Snæfjalladraug*), that he executed by his famous poetry *Snjáfjallavísur*, beginning with this verse:

Far niður, fýla,	Down with your odors,
fjandans limur og grýla;	you extremity of evil, ugly
troll,	
skal þig jörð skýla,	may the earth cover you
en skreytin aursíla;	and the mud decorate you,
þú skalt eymdir ýla	you shall howl in misery
og ofan eftir stíla,	on your way down where
you belong,	
vesall, snauður víla;	you wretched crying crea-
ture,	
þig villi óheilla brýla.[217]	may you rove astray in the
mist of misfortune	

(Transl. ÓKÞ)

Jón the learned probably never had a choice other than to do what his fellow countrymen expected of him. So he lived up to the expectations about him, thereby fulfilled his image as a ghost buster, and chanted down the Snowy-Mountain Ghost, as well as he delivered paper-pieces with magical-signs for healing along with some good advice. But only very few of his countrymen understood what Jón was all about.

---

216 Gísli Oddsson 1942: Undur Íslands.
217 Jón Guðmundsson 1936, p.85.

The "Nerd" and the Folklorist

Jón Guðmundsson developed his artistic skills by his poetry, by hand-constructing, painting and drawing – for example remarkable church-decorations that have been preserved. His studies and researches embraced science of nature, study of old runes, folklore and ethnological knowledge. In fact Jón Guðmundsson deserves to be appointed as the first Icelandic folklorist and ethnologist. But he had one more role in life, still not mentioned. He had a journalistic role – as a writer and speaker of truth.

.Jón's methods of research are worth mentioning. His methods were encyclopedic in such a scale that he himself may be described as an *encyclopediac* – even though that is not a word to be found in a dictionary, it may be the only correct concept there is to analyze his scholarly working methods.

For Jón the learned a phenomena had several layers of existence and meaning, and he would try to unveil all these layers while describing and analyzing that particular item. His thesis "A Brief Description of the Diverse Natures of Iceland" (*Stutt undirrétting um Íslands aðskiljanlegar náttúrur*) contains examples of this. Describing the animals, a whale or a seal for example, he would draw a picture, describe the physical characteristics, tell about the folk-belief connected to this particular being, mention its way of living, its function in nature etc. His scholarly works were what we Icelanders call *samtíningur*, a gathering of various fragments of wisdom, somewhat an interesting mixture of observations and folklore. Therefore some scholars of the 19th and early 20th centuries – albeit giving him some credit for his contribution – considered Jón Guðmundsson to have been some kind of a weirdo, claiming for instance that he was "a strange item of catholic-Lutheran folklore-blend" (*kynlegt dæmi um samruna kaþólskra og lútherskrar hjátrúarskoðana*),[218] that he was "spiteful, eccentric, superstitious and catholic" (*heiptugr í skapi, sérvitr og fullr hjátrúar, og pápískr í trú*).[219] Those scholars, as many of their 19th

---

218 Páll Eggert Ólason 1942, p. 255.
219 Guðbrandur Vigfússon 1962, p. xi.

and 20th century colleagues, were of course blinded by the sharp illumination of the new age of science. Therefore they ignored the fact that Jón the learned did not live in an established scientific atmosphere. His paradigm was played out by his own interest and enthusiasm for observing, learning and discovering life's wonders and to present them to others. He was a "nerd" in the best sense of that word.

This enthusiasm of Jón Guðmundsson made him unique, even though we know of few others like him: Men like Magnús Hjaltason (the scald from Þröm 1873-1916), Þórður Þórðarson from Grunnavík (1878-1913) and Sighvatur (Grímsson) Borgfirðingur (1840-1930), even Gísli Konráðsson (1787-1877) who got his first support as a scholar when he had reached the age of 70. All of them were scholars in their own right, in spite of poverty and lack of formal education, studying and writing, producing amounts of written knowledge, some of them against all odds without support from institutions or individuals.

In Iceland the 17th century was a time of ignorance and sorcery-fear, a time when punishment was the answer to all misdoings, when misuse of power was rather a rule than an exception and justice as such only premature, as has been argued splendidly by Árni Magnússon and Páll Vídalín in their rapport about the Icelandic justice system of the 17th century.[220] Therefore one can easily argue that Jón the learned was unfortunate to exist at times hostile to his skills and innate characteristics. He didn't fit in at all. Too educated for the common public – too powerless and disobedient for the authorities.

It is remarkable though that Jón's very few soulmates were highly educated men of high and formal social status, men like Brynjólfur Sveinsson bishop in Skálholt who tried to have Jón write more about the Icelandic runes, and Ole Worm, a Danish professor at the University of Copenhagen, who tried to assist Jón while the latter was running his legal errands in Denmark after having been convicted as a sorcerer and expelled from Iceland.[221] It is quite possible that

---

220 Árni Magnússon og Páll Vídalín 1916: Embedsskrivelser og andre offentlige aktstykker, Copenhagen.
221 Jón Halldórsson 1911-1915, p. 87; Breve fra og til Ole Worm III, p. 397.

these two men, bishop Brynjólfur and professor Worm, were the reason why Jón did not end up at the burning-stake. Burning at the stake could easily have become his fate, had he not had a few powerful friends as counterweight against the powerful enemies he had aroused.

The Journalist and the Whistle Blower

As a scholar Jón the learned deserves to be appointed as the first folklorist of Iceland. As a writer he deserves to be appointed as the first journalist – or even the first whistle blower.

Today the media is believed to be the fourth power of society. By means of journalism **nerds** and **whistle blowers** can have huge influence in society by unveiling knowledge to the public, and therefore undermine the authority of established institutions such as the very governments. In a way Jón the learned had a similar function. He stirred up the water waves under the boat, causing uneasiness of his governors. Both spiritual and secular authorities disliked the influence he had on the common people of Iceland, not least when he started to present the ugly truth about the "Slaying of the Spaniards" to his countrymen.

Therefore, to describe the man, Jón the learned Guðmundsson, one has got to distinguish between three categories of his being: His image or identity – his occupation – and his actual function.

Image / Identity	Occupation	Function
Power poet	Artist (Poet, Painter)	„Nerd"
Ghost buster	Hand constructer Writer	„Journalist" (Whistle blower)
Healer	„Scholar"	Folklorist Ethnologist

Jón's **image** or even his **identity** was the one of a ghost-buster as well as the one of a power-poet, the healer and maybe even the sorcerer. His **occupation** was the one of the artist as well as the one of the scholar – he was a writer, a poet, a collector and a man of science albeit premature. His **function** was the one of a folklorist and ethnologist – but more importantly for his fate, he had a journalistic role.

In spite of his poverty and lack of social status Jón the learned had one particular power, and that was only partial the power of knowledge because only very few understood the meaning of his knowledge. His strongest power was the urge for telling the truth – even greater a threat because he had the braveness to speak out. His powerful instrument was his skill of writing which ensured his power of speech to spread out the truth. This is why the upper class and formal authorities of 17th century Iceland tended to undermine Jón Guðmundsson the learned and have him put aside. It was his credibility and his popularity that had to be dealt with – therefore the accusation of witchcraft, and the slander planted around him.

His life-story turned out as a classic example of so many others in his position at all times: The story of a speaker of truth who became an outcast.

References

Alþingisbækur Íslands V, 160-1639. Sögufélag. Reykjavík 1922.

Árni Arnarson 1996: „Náttvíg Íslands". Morgunblaðið – Lesbók. 13. Jan., 2. tbl. P. 1-2.

Árni Arnarson 1996: „Náttvíg Íslands II. Ari býst í stríð". 20. jan. 3 tbl., p. 10-11.

Árni Magnússon og Páll Vídalín 1916: *Embedsskrivelser og andre offentlige aktstykker.* Kristian Kålund annaðist útgáfuna. Copenhagen.

Breve fra og til Ole Worm, I-III. Translated by H.D. Schepelern and Holger Friis Johansen. Copenhagen 1965-68.

Davíð Ólafsson 2003: "Skrifaður í köldum og óhentugum sjóbúðum …
" Sighvatur Grímsson Borgfirðingur og miðlun bókmenningar
á Vestfjörðum á síðari hluta 19. aldar. Vestfirðir, aflstöð íslen-
skrar sögu. Ársrit Sögufélags Ísfirðinga, 43, p. 229-243.

Einar Gunnar Pétursson 1998: *Eddurit Jóns Guðmundssonar lærða.* Samantektir um skilning á Eddu og að fornu í þeirri gömlu norrænu
kölluðust rúnir bæði ristingar og skrifelsi. Þættir úr fræðasögu
17. aldar. Stofnun Árna Magnússonar á Íslandi. Reykjavík.

Finnur Sigmundsson 1951 (bjó til prentunar): Úr fórum Jóns
Árnasonar. Sendibréf II. Reykjavík.

Gísli Oddsson 1942: *Íslenzk annálabrot (annalium in Islandia farrago); Undur
Íslands (De mirabilibus Islandiæ.* [Jónas Rafnar translated]. Þorste-
inn M. Jónsson. Akureyri.

Guðmundur Einarsson: Hugrás (Manuscript) Lbs 404 8vo.

Gunnar M. Magnúss 1973: Ósagðir hlutir um skáldið á Þröm. Ævisaga
Magnúsar Hj. Magnússonar skrifara. Skuggsjá. Hafnarfjörður.

Halldór Hermannsson 1924: *Jón Guðmundsson and his Natural History of
Iceland.* Islandica – an annual relating to Iceland and the Fiske
Icelandic Collection in Cornell University Library. Vol. 15.
Ithaca, NY : Cornell University Library.

Hannes Þorsteinsson (unpublished): Æfir lærðra manna. [ÞÍ HÞ Æfir].

Hjörleifur Guttormsson (ritstjóri) 2013: Í spor Jóns lærða. Hið íslenska
bókmenntafélag. Reykjavík.

Jón Halldórsson 1911-1915. *Biskupasögur Jóns prófasts Halldórssonar í Hítar-
dal með viðbæti.* 2. bindi. Hólabiskupar 1551-1798. (Sögurit II).
Sögufélag. Reykjavík.

Jón Guðmundsson 1916: *Fjölmóður.* Ævidrápa Jóns lærða Guðmundssonar með inngangi og athugasemdum eftir Pál Eggert Ólason
> *Safn til sögu Íslands* V, p. 1-92.

Jón Guðmundsson: „Stutt undirrétting um Íslands aðskiljanlegar náttúrur" > Halldór Hermannsson 1924: Islandica 15.

Jón Guðmundsson 1936: Snjáfjallavísur hinar síðari í móti þeim síðara gangára á Snæfjöllum 1612. Jón Þorkelsson bjó til útgáfu. *Huld* II. Safn alþýðlegra fræða íslenzkra (Önnur útgáfa), p. 85-94.

Jónas Kristjánsson (bjó til prentunar) 1950: *Spánverjavígin 1615*. Sönn frásaga eftir Jón Guðmundsson lærða og Víkingarímur. Hið íslenzka fræðafjelag. Kaupmannahöfn

Már Jónsson 2015: "The Killings of 1615. Antecedents and Plausible Causes." *Basque Whaling in Iceland in the XVII Century*. Editor: Irujo, Xavier. University of California, Santa Barbara, p. 139-151.

Oddur Einarsson 1971: Íslandslýsing. Qualiscunque descriptio Islandiae. [Sveinn Pálsson translated] Menningarsjóður. Reykjavík.

Ólína [Kjerulf] Þorvarðardóttir 2000: *Brennuöldin. Galdur og galdratrú í málskjölum og munnmælum*. Háskólaútgáfan. Reykjavík.

Ólína [Kjerulf] Þorvarðardóttir 2013: "Í spor Jóns lærða". Bókarumsögn. Ársrit Sögufélags Ísfirðinga 2013, p. 53.

Páll Eggert Ólason 1916 (ritaði inngang og athugasemdir) > Jón Guðmundsson lærði: *Fjölmóður*.

Páll Eggert Ólason 1942: *Saga Íslendinga* V. Seytjánda öld. Reykjavík.

Safn til sögu Íslands og íslenzkra bókmenta að fornu og nýju I-V. Kaupmannahöfn/Reykjavík 1856-1929.

Sigurður Gylfi Magnússon (tók saman) 1997: *Bræður af Ströndum. Dagbækur, ástarbréf, almenn bréf, sjálfsævisaga, minnisbækur og samtíningur frá 19. öld*. Háskólaútgáfan. Reykjavík.

Viðar Hreinsson 1996: "Tvær heimsmyndir á 17. öld. Snorra Edda í túlkun Jóns Guðmundssonar lærða (1574-1658). *Guðamjöður og arnarleir. Safn ritgerða um Eddulist*. Háskólaútgáfan. Reykjavík, p. 117-163.

CHAPTER EIGHT

Jón Guðmundsson lærði's "Sönn frásaga" and its repercussions on his life. His stay on Snæfellsnes and his reputation there and later.

Einar G. Pétursson

The late Jónas Kristjánsson, director of the Árni Magnússon Institute in Reykjavík, published a volume titled *Slaying of the Spaniards* (Spánverjavígin 1615) in 1950. It contained the primary sources about that event, including Jón Guðmundsson the Learned's work *A true account of the shipwreck and slaughter of the Spaniards* (Sönn frásaga af spanskra skipbrotum og slagi). Jónas Kristjánsson thought the *True account* was written the winter after the slaying, 1615–1616. There are no accounts of the reasons why Jón composed the work, though it is possible that it was meant to be a document to be used in legal proceedings that followed the event. It is extremely likely that it was composed due to some external influence, rather than mere desire on Jón's part to record the event. However, much documentation from this period has been lost because of the Copenhagen fire of 1728. Luckily for us, in 1649 Jón the Learned composed an autobiographical poem called *Fjölmóður,* in which he refers to the event. I will give a brief account of the life of Jón the learned and of his major writings prior to the slaying of the Spaniards in 1615. Additional information about Jón and his writings can be found in my work *Eddurit Jóns Guðmundssonar lærða* from 1998 and in Í spor Jóns lærða from 2013. Jón was born in Ófeigsfjörður in Strandir in 1574. He grew up in a bookish family.

He spent most of his youth with his grandfather, Hákon Þormóðsson, and his paternal uncle Jón Hákonarson. A manuscript of *rímur,* written by or for a man called Jón Hákonarson, is preserved in Stockholm, and it has been suggested that the owner was Jón's uncle. A comparison of readings in these *rímur* with texts of the same *rímur* in the works of Jón the Learned strongly suggest that he knew the manuscript.

Jón's maternal grandfather was a priest, and therefore literate; Jón knew him as a child. In short, Jón grew up among people who had been educated before the Reformation. They appear to have resented the change of faith; Jón's writings to the Lutheran bishop, Brynjólfur Sveinsson, show more indignation against the Reformation than might be thought prudent.

Jón began to copy books at an early age. In 1592, when he was 18, he made a copy of the A version of the *Saga of Bishop Guðmundr Arason* to which he added accounts of miracles from the B version of the saga. At that time it was not common to copy medieval texts, and the story of Guðmundur did not correspond well with Lutheran theology. He also copied a gospel book from a printed book with ordinary printed letters, but Jon's copy contains decorated initials, some using colored ink. The letter forms in this book are based on foreign models, which have, however, not been identified.

Jón the learned spent the years 1605–11 at Skarð on Skarðsströnd, where he saw a vellum book containing the sagas of the Apostles, the famous Skarðsbók. He also mentions that he saw other books and documents there. In addition to his copying and decorating books, Jón was famous for his painting and carving of walrus ivory (he was often called 'Jon the painter' or 'Jón the carver') and probably did this sort of work while at Skarð.

From Skarð Jón travelled north to Strandir, where he exorcized ghosts at Staður on Snæfell in the years 1611 and 1612. Jón's first known original compositions are poems against ghosts (Icelandic 'draugar,' animated corpses rather than mere spirits). The first poem, *Fjandafæla*, (in English 'Demon Deterrent') is preserved in many manuscripts. It is among the longer surviving exorcism poems and was considered particularly powerful against ghosts; I´ll return to its contents later.

After Jón refused to be part of the attack on the Spaniards in 1615 he fled south to Snæfellsnes towards the end of the winter 1616 and stayed there until 1627. The leader of the attack on the Spaniards was the sheriff Ari Magnússon of Ögur. Jón frequently referred to the fact that he and his wife were plundered of their possessions, among other things books and valuable stones; Ari must have thought that they would not be able to succeed in a legal case against him.

On Snæfellsnes Jón was protected by the sheriff Steindór Gís-lason, who was first cousin to the wife of Ari of Ögur. Ari was also the son-in-law of Bishop Guðbrandur Þorláksson of Hólar. Soon after arriving on Snæfellsnes, Jón sent his son, Guðmundur, to the school run by Bishop Guðbrandur at Hólar, and it is clear that he was held in high esteem in those quarters.

What was Jón's position like on Snæfellsnes? Research in recent years had shown unambiguously that he enjoyed high esteem as a scholar, much more than was believed earlier. The most important of such research is the conclusion of Ólafur Halldórsson in his book *Grænland í miðaldaritum* published in 1978 that Jón lærði composed *Grænlands annál* in 1623. That work only survives in a revised version by Björn Jónsson of Skarðsá. The annals made use of extracts from the manuscript *Hauksbók* which was written around 1300.

Grænlands annál was composed for the intellectuals at Hólar, most likely for Þorlákur Skúlason who at that time was schoolmaster but later became bishop. In the same year, 1623, Þorlákur Skúlason sent a runic alphabet to the Danish doctor Ole Worm, which he said he had obtained from the man who was most knowledgeable about runic letters. He didn´t mention who the individual was, but since Jón's knowledge of runes is referred to elsewhere, it is extremely likely that he is the source of the alphabet. Worm's path was to cross Jón's later on. It is also important to mention one of Jón's works, *Um nokkrar grasanáttúrur, (Herbarium)*, which contains medical advice that was used when Bishop Guðbrandur of Hólar was ill in the years 1624 to 1627. It is most natural to assume that the people at Hólar had sought his advice concerning the bishop's illness.

It was not only the scholars at Hólar with whom Jón had contact during his stay on Snæfellsnes. In his work *Tíðfordríf* he mentions that Árni, son of Bishop Oddur Einarsson of Skálholt, had shown him a letter about a marriage in Greenland in the year 1408. The letter is only preserved in copies made in 1625 for Bishop Oddur. The letters are not mentioned in *Grænlands annál*. It seems likely that Jón and Árni had met, and Árni had indicated to Jón what he thought was missing in *Grænlands annál*. Jón the Learned also mentions that he lent Árni old and new medical books. These references show that Jón had a reputation as a healer, and strengthens the opinion that his aid was sought when Bishop Guðbrandur was ill. It is clear that during his years on Snæfellsnes, Jón enjoyed a high reputation in the centers of learning at Skálholt and Hólar.

It is worth pausing to mention an interesting passage in *Grænlands annál*, which states that Snorri Sturluson "added to the Edda that the priest Sæmundur the Wise had previously composed." This is the oldest source for the claim that Sæmundur the Wise composed an 'Edda'. Other seventeenth-century scholars followed Jón in this belief, for example Magnús Ólafsson of Laufás, who at first knew of no Edda other than Snorri's, but later changed his mind. Arngrímur the Learned and Bishop Brynjólfur Sveinsson were also of the same opinion. Bishop Brynjólfur's ideas appear clearly in a famous reference, in the commentary on Saxo Grammaticus, *Notæ uberiores*, by Stephanus Johan Stephanius from the year 1645, concerning a lost Edda of Sæmundr the Wise. We don´t know where Jón got the idea about an Edda by Sæmundr, but most likely it was an oral tradition during his lifetime, when much was attributed to Sæmundr. At any rate, the spread of the attribution shows that people valued Jón's opinion.

As I mentioned earlier, the first surviving writing by Jón is his exorcism poem, *Fjandafæla*, from 1611. *Fjandafæla* itself caused great controversy. In 1627 the priest Guðmundur Einarsson of Staðarstað composed a work called *Hugrás* to refute it, and counted up eight 'ungodly teachings' it contained — by which he meant teachings that did not correspond to Lutheran orthodoxy. He poured scorn on its claims, providing learned arguments against them. Some of the statements to which he took objection were "that a tenth of the angels were originally supposed to serve Lucifer," or the third, "that there are three heavens up to the moon, and another three above that." The sixth claim is that "a great squadron of angels accompanied Christ to hell to do battle to the devils, and rescued the patriarchs who were imprisoned there." This is just a sample of the teachings that are mentioned in *Hugrás*. Where did Jón learn these heretical ideas? They will hardly have been oral traditions from Strandir, they must derive from some lost book to which Jón had access at a young age.

Following the discussion of the 'heretical' information in *Fjandafæla* is a "Short answer to the double opposition we all receive, who question the forbidden art of healing." The 'art' consisted, according to magicians, of using powerful prayers, magical staves, and poems like *Fjandafæla* to drive away the devil, though Guðmundur's conclusion, expressed in no uncertain terms, was that *Fjandafæla* was more likely to attract devils than deter them.

Hugrás was composed in 1627, the same year that Bishop Guðbrandur Þorláksson of Hólar died. We may ask whether the priest would have dared to write against Jón before he learned that Guðbrandur was dead? *Hugrás* not only addressed heretical claims in *Fjandafæla*, but also mentions the contents of grimoires. Much of their contents has parallels in a booklet that called down a condemnation for witchcraft on Jón in 1631. In *Hugrás* Guðmundur says nothing about the authors of the grimoires, and it has often been claimed, incorrectly, that they were by Jón Guðmundsson. Such booklets were often copied from each other and resembled each other so closely that it is inappropriate to speak of an individual author. Guðmundur went on to say that magicians were shown excessive lenience in Iceland. He then quoted a royal letter from 1617 about the use of occult arts, including "signings, exorcisms, runes, magical symbols". This was considered to be "a provocation and abomination against God". He pointed out that overseas, witches and magicians were burned, and reproaches the sheriffs for neglecting such things. In *Hugrás,* Guðmundur is very excited and it must be concluded that he was responsible for Jón's moving south to Akranes, where he stayed with Árni Gíslason, lögréttumaður at Ytri-Hólmur, the brother of Sheriff Steindór who had protected Jón on Snæfellsnes.

In 1628 Guðmundur, Jón's son, was ordained priest and appointed to the church of Hvalsnes in Miðnes; Jón then lived with him. However, the reverend Guðmundur became entangled in legal dealings with Ólafur Pétursson, steward of the governor, with the result that Guðmundur was removed from office in 1630. That same year, Jón was declared an outlaw by Ólafur Pétursson at a local assembly, and suffered many other afflictions. The next year, 1631, Jón appealed his case to the National Assembly and was not found guilty, but was taken to Bessastaðir, the governor's residence, and condemned to outlawry on the first of August, 1631. The damning evidence was a pamphlet called *Bót eður viðsjá við illu ákasti* (Remedy and Prevention of Evil Attacks), of which thirty topics are listed. It contains a variety of remedies, including charms and spells, many of which people would not have thought twice about using. It was about this time that Magnús Ólafsson of Laufás wrote to Ole Worm that Jón the learned was extremely knowledgeable about runes. After the trial, Jón went to the Eastfjörds. In 1636 he and his son, Guðmundur, went to Copenhagen and Jón presented his case to the University Council, where it was heard by the rector, none other than Ole Worm. A pamphlet, probably with similar material to the one presented in his case at Bessastaðir, was presented in evidence. Jón said that the contents were papistic heresy.

The conclusion of the trial was that the case was sent back to the National Assembly, where the original sentence was confirmed and Jón was sent to the East in 1627 to stay there until the end of his life in 1658. It was there that he wrote his most important works for Bishop Brynjólfur Sveinsson, many of which were material for the bishop's intended study of ancient Nordic religion, which however was never completed. In 1641 Jón copied and wrote a commentary on Snorri's Edda titled *Samantektir um skilning á Eddu* (Compilations on Understanding the Edda) based on a now lost manuscript. For same purpose he wrote a commentary on *Brynhildarljóð* from the text of *Völsunga saga*. On the same poem Björn Jónsson of Skarðsá also wrote a commentary. It was before bishop Brynjólfur Sveinsson got the only manuscript of the Older Edda. As a sort of continuation of *Samantektir*, Jón composed *Tíðfordríf* for Bishop Brynjólfur. I have been attempting to write a commentary on it for an intended edition, but it had been very difficult. Jón's learning is so great that the contents are such that Latin scholars and Professors of Theology are equally at a loss for explanations.

From this brief summary it is clear that there is much learning in Jón's oldest writings; when on Snæfellsnes he wrote *Grænlands annál* for the scholars at Hólar, a work which had great influence. At that time he was also in contact with scholars in Skálholt. In his final years in eastern Iceland the most learned man in Iceland, Bishop Brynjólfur Sveinsson, asked him for explanations of Nordic mythology and many other learned matters. Jón was one of a group of scholars who wrote for the bishop, and at least some of what he wrote was also known at Hólar. This shows that his account of the Slaying of the Spaniards and the accusation of sorcery did not affect his high reputation as a scholar.

CHAPTER NINE

The "Basque sea" in 17th-18th century texts

Aurélie Arcocha-Scarcia
(Université Michel Montaigne, IKER-UMR 5478)
Mari Jose Olaziregi
(University of the Basque Country/Etxepare Basque Institute)

Goazen eta pasa detzagun	Go and take on
Tromenta harrigarriak;	the Scary storm;
Bertze Munduak bilhatzagun	Seek other worlds
Eta itsaso berriak	And new seas

GASTELUÇAR Bernard (1686)

Although it might sometimes have been the case that whales were hunted and captured in the Bay of Biscay, two in Biarritz in 1615, for example (EE Bundle 87), and another in 1625 (EE 88 Bundle) as evidenced in the Baiona archives, for the most part whaling and cod fishing required undertaking long and arduous voyages to distant areas of the European Northland, to the "Ice Island" where we are now, but also beyond, to Greenland, and to Spitsbergen. One document mentions that sailors from Lapurdi went "on whaling in the seas of Greenland and Norway" around the years 1607-1622 (EA 87 Roll, Library of Bayonne). However, most of the ships left the "Sea of the Basques" to anchor along the coast of Newfoundland and the coast of southern Labrador.

Some texts in Basque and French and Spanish, in the 17th and 18th centuries, essentially reflect those dangerous sea voyages of sailors hunting whales, fishing cod off the coast of Newfoundland, the St. Lawrence Estuary, South Labrador ... indicating how whale hunting and cod fishing require specific instruments and distinct and specialized techniques in defined areas. We know that this context is inseparable from the hazards of politics and of wars between different powers. Politics and religion, we should add, as the eight wars of religion that occurred between the years 1562 and 1598 in France had a major impact on the one hand on the production and spread of the religious books, and on the other, sometimes on the navigation book to be sold in the ports of the Atlantic coast.

The aim of this brief presentation will be to reflect on the representation of whale hunting and the maritime world in general in Basque classic texts. And we underline Basque, because we are dealing with a very unknown corpus of texts for the vast majority of scholars who specialize in Basque Studies. Here we have chosen to focus on four areas. Firstly, we will focus quickly on two non-literary texts: the Basque language ship's log by the pilot Captain Pierre Detxeberri, nicknamed 'Dorre', who was also a cartographer for Governor Parat of Placentia in 1698. This not only raises questions about the hypotext written in French which must have inspired "Dorre" as regards the peculiarity of the "translation" he carried out but also about the circulation and spread of the book in the context of Aquitaine where La Rochelle printers who published nautical books had to use clever strategies to make financial profit from selling them, for example, in Bordeaux.

Secondly, we will analyze an archive document in French from 1732 that we will discuss briefly. This document demonstrates at the same time the importance of the harpoon business in whaling in 1732. Official policies and cross-border collaborations could be established when there was a shortage of that specific skill on one and / or the other side of the border (as is the case here with the chronic lack of harpooners on the Labourdin side under the French crown).

Lastly, we will look at specific literary representations that appear in *The series of prayers for the sea* (Bordeaux, 1627), by the religious poet Joanes Etxeberri de Ciboure, and in four manuscripts found in a song book perhaps made by several compilers and / or authors in a stretch of time from 1714 (after the Treaty of Utrecht) until the early 1800s, or in a broader temporal space than just 1789 to which these texts usually refer. As we will contend, the representation of the maritime world in Basque classic texts is necessarily inscribed in a context where other fragments of texts, including those in Basque, meet, including hypotexts like the Odyssey, biblical texts of the Old and New Testament and sacred history, cosmographies and legendary voyages to the lands of the North and West.

The Basque navigation book of Pierre Detxeberri, known as 'Dorre' (Bayonne, 1677).

The Luzien (Donibane Lohizune) navigator Pierre Detcheverry Dorre, was a ship's captain but also a pilot and cartographer for the Governor of Placentia (two maps dated 1689), the existence of which is attested in several archive documents dated 1688 to 1690. He was also the author of a technical nautical book in Basque on navigation (Bayonne, 1677), the layout of which indicates that it is a hypertext previously published in French "by Chouin" and "in Bordeaux", and called Adventurous Travels. It could have been written by a certain Martin Hoiarzabal of Ciboure but we do not know for sure if he existed. Research in the 60s by Eugénie Droz revealed that it is actually a false typographical address, and that the book was printed in reality in Protestant held land by the Huguenot printer Jean Portau.

The book by Pierre Detcheverry "Dorre" is more than just a "translation"; it is also bears witness to geo-political changes in France and Europe since 1589. Because the Treaty of Utrecht in 1714 changed the areas of settlement and fisheries, the south and east coasts would gain favored attention in Dorre's book in Basque while Hoyarzabal draws a Newfoundland geography limited to eastern and southern coasts. Dorre's book was printed and distributed, so it also served an educational purpose, on which we lack data but should investigate further.

A French archives document of 1732 on the "harpoon" profession among Basque sailors

This document is a draft letter. It offers an interesting testimony on the Lapurdi maritime past during the second quarter of the 18th century, especially around 1735. The purpose of the letter is to prevent the arrival of harpooners from Gipuzkoa in French territory to board whaling ships at Saint-Jean-de-Luz and Bayonne from being considered a crime by the Spanish crown, because the economic consequences of this would have been detrimental to trade from the ports of Bayonne and Saint-Jean-de-Luz. Monsieur de Champeaux, Steward of Commerce in Seville, is probably implicitly responsible for initiating several diplomatic representations to the Spanish crown authorities so that a successful outcome could satisfy both parties and could be found via an "agreement of measures" that the inhabitants Bayonne and Saint-Jean-de-Luz wish to make with the people of Gipuzkoa "for employing so-called harpooners and sailors and to not be troubled as they have been in past years."

Such cross-border agreements, also called *conversas* in Spanish, were never definitively stable. The issue of the harpooners is of particular interest to the two parties at a time when the Treaty of Utrecht (1713)[222] left Basque offshore peninsular fishing empty-handed, even when fishing traditions dating back several centuries continued.

We see that, twenty years after the aforementioned Treaty, Gipuzkoan sailors specializing in whaling find employment especially on Labourdin whaling ships, which are also contracted by traders who realize there is growing disaffection toward the harpooning business among their own sailors. The document reveals that the sailors of Labourd prefer, in the second quarter of the eighteenth century, to engage in "more useful" travels, meaning more profitable (and less dangerous), i.e. the cod fishery in Newfoundland and off Île Royale (Cape Breton or Royal Isle), and that of the fur trade with native peoples that seems to especially attract officers. The writer suggests a shortage of men: "The Department of Bayonne and S. Jean de Luz cannot provide enough sailors to equip all whaling vessels that sail there to Newfoundland" and mentions plans to recruit one hundred and fifty Gipuzkoan harpoon masters "for equipping whaling ships". These figures indicate high rates of production of whale and dried cod oil for the years 1730-1734. Placentia (south of Newfoundland) and Louisburg (capital of Isle Royale) show that this is the heyday of L'Isle Royale business activity.

The writer also seems to think it desirable for the harpooners to have better training in hydrography. We realize, reading the memoirs, that the harpooners form a true caste, a very close-knit corporation enjoying privileged treatment that also results in very high wages. The huge financial stakes as well as the ex-

---

222 The Treaty of Utrecht had unequal consequences on both sides of the border. They were indeed much less catastrophic for Labourdins as France managed to maintain "the exclusive privilege of fishing in the eastern part of the coast from Cape Bonavista to the most western point, and from there to Cape Riche, on the west coast. The treaty forbade our nation to fortify any point on land or erect any other buildings than fishermen's huts and the necessary fishing scaffolds. In addition, they could stay on the island past the time for drying cod. "(Ducere 1893: 4 -5). But there was nothing like this for the Basques of Gipuzkoa and Bizkaia, since the Spanish crown lost all its fishing rights on the island. (Ciriquiain Gaztiarro: 313-328).

treme danger of this business explain the benefits given to them. Each training session is highly specialized with "in the field" learning that starts early and lasts several years, and it is clear that even carpenters and coopers have virtually no chance to move from one business to another. To be a harpooner, you start by boarding whaling ships as a simple sailor with "very mediocre gains". After several "Whale voyages" or to the North of Europe, to Greenland and Spitzbergen as noted above or to the coast of North America, the sailors who sail on the boats have the opportunity to gain valuable experience. Of the eight men who make up the crew of the rowboat, the harpooner, accompanied by his trusted man, the master of the rowboat, has the opportunity to observe the six rowers and identify the best ones. The boat masters are always former rowers and former harpoon boat masters. The author of the report accurately describes the harpooner's stance, harpoon in hand, and the key role held by his second. The writer concludes the paragraph by comparing whaling and "Bull Running": If the harpooner is omnipresent in this historical text, he is also often drawn or engraved, and he also appears as the central character in three texts by the Baroque poet Etxeberri of Ziburu.

Prayers for sea travel

Joannes Etxeberri Ciboure is certainly the author who gives the most space to the sea in seventeenth-century Basque letters, as a small book of his devotes 31 pages divided into ten chapters (93 texts) to the topic: "The series of prayers for sea travel "(second part of *Devotion Manual*, 1627). It is therefore necessary to insert the three texts on whaling within this entire corpus dedicated to the maritime world. The harpooner intervenes after the immobilization of the whale. Protected by the heavenly powers, his stance is sure and perfect. The verses of Joanes Etxeberri express the colossal force confronting the harpooner like a new David in the face of Goliath, and the other men of the whaling boat that can do nothing against the "big fish" without the help of God. Rhythmic vivacious scenes accentuate the dramatic tension pushed to extremes:

Etxeberri from Ciboure « Prayers for sea travel » (1627) (chapter IX)

Balea zaleentzat

O Iaun Tobias gaztea ungi begiratua,
Guardaritzat bidaldurik Arkangelu Saindua.
Eta kostara arraña erakharrarazia,
Haren hilltzeko egiten ziñoela grazia.
Guri ere ekharguzu hurbillera Balea,
Segurkiago armaren landatzeko kolpea.
Biziaren gatik dugu hirriskatzen bizia,
Arren egiguzu haren gelditzeko grazia.

For the whalers

Oh Lord, who hath protected young Tobias so well,
In sending him the Holy Archangel as a guardian,
And who hath drawn the fish towards the coast,
Do him the honour that he might kill it.
Lead the whale towards us too,
So that we might strike our weapon more assuredly.
In order to live, we risk our lives,
Do us the honour of restraining it.

Balea kolpatu eta

Iauna geure arte baño gehiago zureaz,
Balea zauritu dugu arpoñaren kolpeaz.
Arren bada egiguzu (Iaun puxanta) grazia,
Sarri gelditzeko arrain itsasoko handia.
Gutarik garabik zaurtxu gabe bere indarraz,
Segadetan dabillala buztan edo bulharraz.
Edo xalupa irauli gabe gillaz gañera,
Edo berekin eraman gabe urtan behera.
Arren begira gaitzatzu gaitz hauk guztietarik,
Eskerra diezazugun itzul lehorrerarik.
Irabazia da handi, perilla ere handia,
Begira diezazugu prinzipalki bizia.

After having wounded the whale

Lord, more for your part than for ours,
We have wounded the whale with a harpoon strike.
Make it so (all powerful Lord), by your grace,
That we soon restrain the big fish of the sea
Without it harming any of us,
While a prisoner in the ropes, it flaps
his tail and sides vigorously.
Or without it turning the keel of the boat skywards,
Or taking us with it beneath the water.
Protect us from all these evils,
So that, once back on dry land, we might thank you.
Great is the gain, great too the peril,
May you watch out, above all, for our lives.

Chapter VII is devoted exclusively to the storm. The adopted structure evokes the gradual rise of the storm from the pre-storm calm
until it eventually abates. All the senses are engaged, the rhetorical
device emphasizes the upward and downward movement and contrast, most of the binary time, size, light, intensity, sound.

Etxeberri from Ciboure «Prayers for sea travel» (1627) (chapter VII)

**Untzia bera galtzeko perillean dabillanean
jendeak salborik promesa**
Iauna urrikal bekizu othoi gure suspira,
Eta untzia ezazu xehatzetik begira.
Geure nekez eta izerdiz irabazi mojanak,
Begira dietzagutzu hor barrena emanak.
Eta hala egiguzu grazia Iongoikoa,
Perill handitik untzia salbo ikhustekoa.
Hartara othoitz egizu **zuk ere o Birjina,**

198

Baita zuk ere halaber untziaren Patroña.
Orobat zuk ere egizu Xabier famatua,
Perilletik dakusagun unzia guardatua.
Eta zuk Iainkoa hekin laudatzatzu othoitzak,
Eta alegeratzatzu gure triste bihotzak.
Egiten badorokuzu eske gauden dohaña,
Bozik darotzugu esker itzuliren ordaña.

The promise when people are saved
while the ship is in danger of being lost
Lord take pity, by your grace, on our breath,
And protect our ship from being destroyed.
The goods earned by our labour and our sweat,
Which are inside the hold, preserve them.
And so, God most high, by your grace,
Let us see the ship saved from great peril.
To this end, may you, too, oh Virgin Mary, pray,
And you, too, patron saint of the ship.
Likewise, you, famed Xavier,
Make it so that our ship may be kept out of peril.
And you, Lord, lend them your prayers,
And brighten our sad hearts,
If you give us the gift we ask for,
We will be pleased to return our due [gratitude]

The longest and most dramatic chapter of maritime poems ends
on a bottom-up structure, of an "anabasique" kind that focuses on
salvation. Ultimately, we can say the same for the whole corpus as
the entire Manual. The poet Joanes Etxeberri closes the last verses
of Chapter X, addressing the sailor-reader that he encourages to
pray under the operating virtue of prayer:

Itsasoko othoitzen zarratzea.
Othoitz hauk xehero tiat ordenatu hunela,
Haukin erratera orhoit dadintzat mariñela.
Perill izigarriari itzurtzeko bezala,
Esker itzultzeko ere minzatu nauk ahala.
Hartarakotz itsasotik illkhi eta salboa,
Esker milla itzul etzak gizon itsas hauzoa.
Orhoit adi zenbat aldiz Iaunak auen guardatu,
Merezitu dukelarik Itsasoan hondatu./(...).

Closing prayers for the sea.
Look, I ordered so carefully these prayers
For the mariner to remember to recite.
I've talked about how to escape the peril,
And as much as possible of how to give thanks.
So, you who escaped the sea and was rescued,
You, sailor, give great thanks.
Remember how many times the Lord has saved you,
While you deserved to spoil thee in the sea./(...)

The perils of the sea and the deep way voyage to Newfoundland

The following texts, which are part of a manuscript corpus contained in the songbook (MS 97) of the Basque Museum of Bayonne, were chosen for their iconic nature. A set entitled *Perils of the Sea*, a trilogy of poems on the journey to Newfoundland, then *The Hardships of Sarrance* vessel en route to Newfoundland. A linear reading of the trilogy is possible but it seems that we move towards an independent reading of each of the three texts that compose it and which are nevertheless linked by the same theme. The writer who wrote the Table of Contents appears to have adopted this view as he brings together the three texts under the unique title of

Hardships of Newfoundland with pagination "from page 1 up to 11". The songbook where these texts are found probably dates from several decades prior to 1798 and has its own entry therein. We could put them in a historical context from the late seventeenth century to the Treaty of Paris, which marked the end of the Seven Years' War (1763). Newfoundland is mentioned but no port is cited. It may well be that it was written after the loss of Piacenza (1713) and during the early years of the nineteenth century, since Labourdins were still going to the ports on the west coast of Newfoundland at that time.

The first of the three texts, *The sad start*, evokes going to Newfoundland in the spring. After the conventional pathos of farewells on the dock, just the mention of the fate of the hazardous sailing promised certain death. The second, *The perils of the sea*, describes a storm during a North Atlantic crossing. Ship and sailors are here doomed to extinction in the black waters that close again completely on them, sealing their fate like that of Ulysses or Dante's Inferno. The text has the structure of a katabasis: death at sea is equivalent to falling into the infernal abyss with no possible redemption. The third text, *Hardships of Newfoundland*, speaks of exiled Basque fishermen (apparently of cod fishermen), assimilated to the damned, from late spring to late summer on the hostile land of Ternua inhabited by wild beasts and human beasts (*giza-bestiak*), the "Eskimos" cannibals. The island of the infernal place, Newfoundland, is the antithesis of the heavenly home of Labourd. The sea crossing is immediately represented as a risky and dangerous journey. The sea is another element whose crossing is treated as an event with an uncertain outcome: "Long is the way to Newfoundland / immense sea that leads to it".

The song *Zarrantzako Penak* tells the story of a boat, the Sarrance, which took two months to reach the port of Placentia in Newfoundland. The subject of the individual experience, which is, according to the context of the master or the commander of the boat, alternates with us from the collective involvement and witness. The story gains in truth. Its chronographic structure recalls the segmentation of a diary and adds to the veracity of the events. It is reminiscent of other popular songs of sailors, crops etc. found in European folklore where the event is surrounded by a series of temporal and rhythmic markers that often mark the beginning of the stanza day, month, or even the name of such a saint or holy figure. The facts to which *Zarrantzako Penak* relates must have taken place before the Treaty of Utrecht of 1713, since the Port de Plaisance, which also later became an English possession, was therefore lost for the sailors of Labourd under the French crown. No other old Basque seafaring song has been received with such temporal information, such a wealth of detail, such accents of truth. The aesthetic concern is undeniable. The dramatic events follow a precise gradation. The poem revolves around the trials, carefully dated (February 16, March 3, March 13, March 14, the "eve of St. Joseph," April 19, "Easter Eve", "Easter Day ") following the introductory verse. All dates that will be given later are related to the various phases of the storm and especially its direct consequences on the boat. The boat, the centerpiece, named and personified is where the test begins on March 3 in a war against an "army of winds" Sea ("The whole sea was arming winds"). The story seems to follow an anabasique structure based on the Gospel account of the Passion and Resurrection of Christ.

Conclusion:

The whale harpooner is a heroic figure, a new David facing Goliath, a new Archangel Michael able to defeat the Demon or a new Theseus fighting the Minotaur. Mixed myths underpin the pen of a poet steeped in ancient culture and / or biblical culture. Mr. Champeau does not think in vain of bullfights evoking the Basque harpooners of Gipuzkoa ... The texts of Joannes Etxeberri Ciboure, as well as the Newfoundland songs and Sarrance of Sentences, can be transposed into another Atlantic geography, navigation to Iceland, or to the furthest North Atlantic islands. Real islands that blend with the old myths revived by a multitude of stories sewn together. Basque texts are no exception to the rule. The same biblical or hagiographic episodes are remembered tirelessly in printed books in Basque by all authors when it comes to evoking the storm: Noah and the Flood;

the crossing of the Red Sea (Tartas, 1666); Jonas' story of being thrown overboard and swallowed up by the "big fish"; the Biblical accounts on calming the storm, Jesus walking on water (Axular, 1643), the storm and the shipwreck of St. Paul told in the Acts of the Apostles (Etcheberri Ciboure, 1627); Psalm 14 of the Book of Wisdom, Psalms 18, 69, 104, 107; the St. Ursula sailing trip to the coast of Cornwall (Larreguy, 1777) or holy miracle Claire rescuing sailors from Pisa (Haramboure, 1635). These are the integrating various proverbs mentioned by the Oihenart "parémiologue", including the following then taken by the translator and author of a Basque-French dictionary, Sylvain Pouvreau (1663 - 1665):

Bibliography

ARCOCHA-SCARCIA, Aurélie. *Territoires oubliés de Terre-Neuve. Mémoire des mots, mémoire des mots à travers les routiers maritimes de Hoyarsabal (1579-1633) et Detcheverry Dorre (1677)*, Madrid : UNED Ediciones, 2002.

_____.« Thématique maritime et variations transtextuelles sur le motif de la tempête en mer dans les lettres basques des XVI - XVIIIe siècles. Un exemple emblématique : Çarrantçaco penac –« Les peines du Sarrance ». (Bayonne, Lapurdum no 07, 2002): 7-35.
see http://www.artxiker.ccsd.cnrs.fr last modification : 2006/06/16 - 09:25:33

_____. « La tempête en mer dans la littérature d'expression basque des XVIIème et XVIIIème siècles : quatre textes emblématiques. », (Donostia-Saint-Sébastián, Eusko Ikaskuntza, 2002): 269-278.
see https://www.eusko-ikaskuntza.org/es/publicaciones/colecciones/cuadernos/articulo.php?o=9172

_____. « Deux imprimeurs rochelais du XVIe siècle : Pierre Haultin, imprimeur du Testamentv

Berria (1571) traduit par Jean de Liçarrague, et Jean Portau, imprimeur de l'édition 1579 des Voyages Avantvrevx du Capitaine-Pilote Martin de Hoyarsabal de Ciboure », (Donostia-San Sebastián, Eusko Ikaskuntza, 2001): 53-83. see https://www.euskoikaskuntza.org/es/publicaciones/colecciones/lankidetzan/articulo.php?o=21119

_____.« Une image inédite du harponneur basque à travers un document de 1732 : « Memoire Pour Monsieur de Champeaux Intandant Du Commerce en France, a Seville au sujet des arponeurs », (Bayonne-SSLA, 2001): 99-116.

_____.« Pierre Detcheverry dit «Dorre», pilote et cartographe labourdin du XVIIe siècle traducteur en euskara du routier d'Hoyarsabal de 1579 », in *Autour de Bertrand d'Etchauz*, ed. Pierre Hourmat and Josette Pontet (Bayonne-SSLA, 2000), 57-82.

_____.« Itsassoco biayetaco othoitcen araldea, « La série de prières pour les voyages en mer », de Joannes Etcheberri de Ciboure (1627).» (Bayonne, Lapurdum 04, 1999), 9-40.

see *https://www. lapurdum.revues.org/1527*

BALCOM, B. A. : *The Cod Fishery of Isle Royale*, 1713-58. Ottawa: Parks Canada, 1984.

DESGRAVES, Louis : *Bibliographie des ouvrages imprimés par Simon Millanges 1572 à 1623*. Bordeaux: Société des Bibliophiles de Guyenne, 1951.

DROZ, Eugénie   : *La veuve Berton et Jean Portau 1573-1589*, in *L'Imprimerie à La Rochelle*, t. III, Genève : Librairie E. Droz, 1960.

ELORTZA Gerardo : « Ternuaco oihartzuna euskal olerkigintzan", in *Itsasoa 3* ed. Selma Barkham, Donostia-San Sebastián: Etor,1987.

ETCHEBERRI, Johanes : *Manual Debotionezcoa…, Bordelen, Gvillen Millanges, Erregueren Imprimat çaillearenean*. Bordeaux : Millanges,1627.

HUXLEY – BARKHAM, Selma : *Itsasoa. El mar de Euskalherria. La Naturaleza, el Hombre y su Historia.* San Sebastián : Etor, 1987.

HOYARSABAL, M. : Les Voyages Avantvreux dv Capitaine Martin de Hoyarsabal, habitant de Cubiburu. Contenant les Reigles & enseignemens necessaires à la bonne & seure Nauigation. A Bourdeaux. De l'Imprimerie de Iean Chouin, Bordeaux : Chouin, 1579.

see https://www.http://gallica.bnf.fr/ark:/12148/bpt6k5819382w

OLAZIREGI, Mari Jose (ed). *Basque Literary History.* Reno: Center for Basque Studies, 2012

TURGEON Laurier : *Pêches basques en Atlantique Nord (XVIIe – XVIIIe siècle).* Thèse de 3ème cycle, Bordeaux : Université Bordeaux 3, 1982.

URKIZU, Patri : *Bertso zahar eta berri zenbaiten bilduma (1798).* Durango : Durangoko Udala, 1987.